Sallie Ann Robinson's Kitchen

UNIVERSITY PRESS OF FLORIDA

Florida A&M University, Tallahassee
Florida Atlantic University, Boca Raton
Florida Gulf Coast University, Ft. Myers
Florida International University, Miami
Florida State University, Tallahassee
New College of Florida, Sarasota
University of Central Florida, Orlando
University of Florida, Gainesville
University of North Florida, Jacksonville
University of South Florida, Tampa
University of West Florida, Pensacola

Sallie Ann Robinson's *Kitchen*

Food & Family Lore from the Lowcountry

Sallie Ann Robinson

Photographs by Deborah Whitlaw Llewellyn

University Press of Florida

Gainesville Tallahassee Tampa Boca Raton Pensacola Orlando Miami Jacksonville Ft. Myers Sarasota

Published in the United States of America. Printed in Korea on acid-free paper.

24 23 22 21 20 19   6 5 4 3 2 1

ISBN 978-0-8130-5629-6
Library of Congress Control Number: 2018953651

Photography by Deborah Whitlaw Llewellyn
Food styling by Annette Joseph
Editing by Janice Shay/Pinafore Press

The University Press of Florida is the scholarly publishing agency for the State
University System of Florida, comprising Florida A&M University, Florida
Atlantic University, Florida Gulf Coast University, Florida International
University, Florida State University, New College of Florida, University of
Central Florida, University of Florida, University of North Florida, University
of South Florida, and University of West Florida.

University Press of Florida
2046 NE Waldo Road
Suite 2100
Gainesville, FL 32609
http://upress.ufl.edu

I dedicate this cookbook to all those before me,
starting with my great-great-great-grandparents
Joe Fields (born 1830) and Ceily (Sara) Brown.
I am proud to be the sixth generation of Gullah
and American Indian heritage whose ancestors
gave me a great bloodline with a rich culture
and history that I am thankful for every day.
This book is dedicated to all my people.

Contents

Preface

Feedin a Hungry Soul

I was born and raised on Daufuskie Island off the coast of South Carolina, which, along with other sea islands, was home to African American and Native American people isolated for more than a century. These people are known as the Gullahs.

The word *Gullah* (also known as *Geechee*) refers to an English Creole language dating back several hundred years to when African slaves who grew rice in the marshy lowlands of the southeastern American colonies didn't want their owners to know what they were saying. The word eventually came to describe my people and our way of life.

Because of the island's isolation (electricity didn't come to Daufuskie until 1952; telephones not until 1973), we Gullah evolved and preserved a unique way of life that has few parallels in contemporary American culture.

When I was growing up on 'Fuskie, as we called our island home then and now, life, as my teacher Pat Conroy viewed it, was indeed a miraculous and joy-filled experience. I didn't identify as "Gullah"; my identity was defined by myself, my family, and our good neighbors, all filled with wisdom, faith, kind hearts, and an old-fashioned knowledge hard to find

today. Our lives were governed by dealing with the important things necessary to get us through each day, and our diets by what we could raise or harvest from the land and sea. We took the good with the bad and didn't worry about things that we did not know, could not get, change, or control.

Native folk like us didn't have much, but everyone was always willing to share what they had. And no one minded lending a helping hand in good or bad times: Folks knew that tomorrow was coming, but not before we got through the night.

I have great memories of a time when things seemed simpler, and hard work and good living went hand and hand. Things were clearly not simpler, but to a child growing up in a place that seemed like paradise, who could tell? To me and all my family and friends, growing up on Daufuskie was really the best of times and, after many of us left for jobs, education, or whatever, nothing would ever be the same again like back in dah day.

Some days were harder than others. But those were the times we learned, even more, how to appreciate one another and make do with what we had. If we kids didn't understand something, our folks would sit us down and give us their best know-how. Like Jesus did in the parables, much of that know-how was put into stories so that we would easily understand their meanings and reasons. They knew we needed to be ready when a change or a challenge would inevitably come. When we were kids, we had no idea how soon these changes and challenges would come.

Until I left Daufuskie to live on the mainland to continue my education, I never knew that there were people in this world who were homeless or hungry. Because, on Daufuskie, folks would never let another be witout sumtin to eat. Day was too much food in dah river and woods dat was available.

Today I live on Daufuskie, although the number of Gullah on the island are fewer and fewer. The house I grew up in is abandoned and falling down. Some of our neighbors' houses have disappeared entirely, reclaimed by weather and nature. Some folks who still own property on Daufuskie speak of returning but can't find the time or way to give up their way of life in the city.

I realize now that, to my Gullah folks, all children were more precious than gold. Those folks, by giving me the learning from their past and present, were making me part of their future, too, and that knowledge is precious to me. It was a memorable upbringing that taught me to appreciate what I have and has given me great hope for my own future.

When it came to cooking, Momma knew that besides ingredients, she had to put a whole lot of love in her meals to feed our hungry souls. And that's how I came to enjoy cooking and to learn, hopefully, how to add all the love that went with it.

Come mealtime, Momma would call out to us to come eat. We already knew it was coming because the aroma of good food had connected with our senses, and we would hurry up to finish our work outside. We would race off to the house to wash our hands in a metal basin half full of water (with a piece of Octagon soap—lye soap that was shaped like a rectangle) that always sat on an old bench in a corner of our kitchen.

Once cleaned up, we had to sit and behave at the dinna table, waiting and watching Momma bringing great-smelling food from the kitchen. If we started twitching in our seats or talking too loud, she would give us that look and say, "Hush up and be still. Y'all chillen act like y'all da starve, dares plenty fo yah to eat. And when yah done eat, dares mo work fo yah to do."

So my sisters and I tried to be patient while sitting in our favorite mix-match chair with our jelly jars half filled with water in front of us. Our hands could not touch anything on the table until it was time to eat. Pop would soon arrive and seat himself at the dinna table with us, and then Momma would finally take off her homemade apron and join us.

Not a sound could be heard as Pop looked at us, knowing our bellies were hungry from the hard work. We would bow our heads to say grace, giving thanks for all that great Gullah food we had on our table. For us kids, everything looked and smelled so good and there was never a question of whether we would like Momma's cooking or not. We knew that if we ever said we didn't like some thing, Pop would be quick to say, "Dare would be mo fo someone else, either you eat what is put in front of yah, or go to bed hungry." Pop and Mom wanted us to know that not all kids ate like us.

Right about halfway through dinna, Momma would remind us that she "did not want to hear any fussin about washing dem dishes." We knew our belly would be full and we had to do the dishes and finish with our work before dark—work like bringing in wood for the stove, locking up the chickens for the night, or pumping enough water for the house.

Pop would sometimes come outside and keep his watchful eye on us, making sure that we did our work the way he wanted it done and without shortcuts. If we thought he was not paying attention and didn't do our work the way we were told, Pop would always catch us, but let us go to bed. Then, in the middle of the night, he would wake us up to finish our work right.

To us, it always seemed that Momma and Pop never tired of finding things for us to do regardless of the time of the day. It was as if they had extra energy that we didn't have. As kids we didn't understand that we were learning life lessons from the scolding and hard work. It was only after I became older and left Daufuskie that I realized the great importance of what they were teaching us: how to use our minds and time wisely so that one day we would know how to work smarter, not harder.

Before I became a parent I thought I knew what hard work was from all that we did growing up. But having children of my own, I discovered that the hardest work had just begun, and I had to rely on all that I was taught. I didn't know how much it took to be a parent and keep a family together through struggles. Or how much faith was needed to get through tragedies that all of us face from time to time. Our folks were good at not showing or discussing their difficulties in front of us. Trouble was grown-folks business, and that was how it was kept. Sometimes, no matter what the situation was, they knew that as long as they kept doing their best, everything was going to be alright.

"Count yo blessins," Pop would say, "for da is some folk dat ain't got nuting at all." We never complained because we never missed anything that we didn't have or know about. Growing up in a house that had holes in the roof, no electric light, no running water, and no plumbing inside was not a concern. To us, getting hand-me-down clothes was a treat, and sleeping in a bed with four or five sisters kept us close and warm on cold winter nights. And when the weather was nice and the bugs wasn't out we enjoyed sleeping on the front porch looking up at the stars high in the sky. Or watch lightning bugs fly around by the thousands.

Today some folks never stop to realize that it does not matter where you are from but where you are going. I was formed by native folks' words of wisdom, storytelling, tough love, support, companionship, and lots of great meals.

Daufuskie Island is changing, and, although I don't wish it, there may be a day when the Gullah have disappeared from this place. I wrote this cookbook to help preserve our way of life, and to share Gullah and lowcountry food with everyone. One of the best ways to remember history is to taste it, so I offer these dishes, from my heart to your mouth.

Cookin dah Beenyah Way

Gullah cooking has been the center of my beenyah soul for as long as I can remember, and long before my time. When I was a child, no shortcuts or quick fixes would do or replace what had to be done in the kitchen (nothing is really complicated, unless you decide to skin and musk a raccoon and you don't know where to start—but don't worry, that's not in this cookbook).

Cooking has been considered by Gullah people as a priceless process that never gets old . . . just better. Folks took what little they had and made tasty meals to feed their family and anyone who dropped by. Bones that were almost meatless or fatbacks added flavor and aroma to fresh organic vegetables. Natives spent hours in their fields, or doing many chores around the house, while their pot slow-cooked on a woodstove. For us this was called "cooking a long pot."

My cooking lessons were simple and true: A good cook knows that there ain't but one way to do it and that is to give it dah love while you are cooking. And if you don't have all you need, then you work with what you got. It's called planning. Bringing main ingredients and spices together is gathering, and combining them is connecting. Balancing the mixture by using the right amount is preparing. And when you have completed all of that, it will be time for you to get out your cooking tools, your pots and pans, and set your temperature to your desired heat.

After you have combined all your ingredients and seasonings and placed your dish on top of the stove or in the heated oven for cooking, stay nearby to give it the love it needs to taste the Gullah way. When you are basting and stirring is also when you are connecting the flavor and aroma for tasting, which is the most important part of the process, because this is where you have the last say and are making sure that the meal has your name on it.

My momma didn't believe in rushing a meal, because she knew that patience and loving what you do made all the difference in perfecting a good meal for the ones you love.

Gullah cooking has been passed down through generations from great cooks who never had any schooling or degrees. They learned from paying attention to folk and watching their every move. Cooking is an art of fixing, mixing, texture, aroma, and good taste buds. You will only get out what you put in, so put a smile on your face and feel the magic of combining a mixture of great food and love.

Now, I want you all to remember that when we used to prepare our food back in the day, recipes were not from cookbooks or about counting calories. Recipes were just like our own history, passed down by word of mouth through many generations. Many can tell you that a Gullah person don't need a cookbook, they knows how to cook because it's in their head, and all they need is the tools to prepare the food. That was because, back then, African Americans were not allowed to write or read, and our Native American ancestors didn't have a writing tradition.

Also, counting calories or watching our waistline was not something we worried about, because, come time to eat, a bellyful was a belly full; however, I have tried to cut calorie corners all I could throughout this book. Of course, when I was growing up we worked hard—all day, every day—and we burned off the excess calories . . . certainly a good argument for exercise today. And remember it's not always what you eat that makes you fat, but how much of what you eat and what you do afterward. Our meals came from things we grew in our garden, raised in our yard, hunted from the woods, and caught in the river, ocean, or creeks.

Many things we used were seasonal and weather-based or, since we were on a sea island, actually determined by the phase of the moon and the cycle of tides: high, low, or flood tide.

Timing was of the essence when it came to knowing when we might get the biggest shrimp or crab catch (both among the most important ingredients in Gullah and lowcountry southern cooking), or even the pecan harvest (we had six pecan trees on our land). Some of our meals were not cooked as healthily as we would cook them today; food preparation was based on taste and what was available—not, as I mentioned, calorie count. Nevertheless, our food was very modern in the sense that most of the fruit and vegetables were organic (our island had lots of fruit and nut trees, and berries grew wild along roadsides or near our backyard), and our chickens and pigs, as well as wild game like raccoons and deer, never knew synthetic herbicides and pesticides and were, obviously, free-range. We even used the cooled ash from the wood burned in our stove to sprinkle over our vegetable garden to keep the bugs off. Also, some of our food was cooked much longer than is fashionable today. Try it the Gullah way and see if longer cooking time doesn't add a depth of flavor that is lacking in quickly cooked food.

I learned to cook the beenyah way from the time I could see over our wood-burning stove in a corner of our kitchen. Momma made sure we paid attention to her every word and move, since measurements were never written down and the woodstove temperature was not controlled by knobs. Our way of cooking was pretty much measured by texture, smell, and taste. For these recipes, though, I have given you the benefit of my lifetime of experience with cooking times and ingredient measures and cooking temperatures.

Finally, if there is some ingredient in one of these recipes that you can't eat or don't like, go ahead and use your common sense to improvise. We made do with all the things we had on hand back in the day, because complaining didn't help. If you want crab and rice (page 135) but have only shrimp or oysters on hand, they make a great substitute. So I invite you to treat yourself to some belly-fillin, lip-smackin, down-home beenyah dinnas.

Belly-Fillin Sallets

Pop felt lettuce was rabbit food and couldn't fill our hungry bellies enough after a hard day of work, so our sallets used other ingredients. Momma had ways of preparing many fruit or meat sallets with our meals because she knew they were much more substantial. She also felt we were good as long as we ate lots of other vegetables that we grew in our garden. Our meat sallets were made mostly from leftovers that needed to be used up because we did not throw away any food.

Sea Island Shrimp Sallet

This cold seafood salad is great as an appetizer, a main dish, or for your next picnic.

Serves 6 to 8

1 teaspoon salt, or more to taste

1 teaspoon pepper, or more to taste

2 pounds large raw shrimp, peeled and deveined

½ onion, chopped

1 pinch chopped fresh dill (optional)

1 tablespoon diced pimento (optional)

½ rib celery, diced

¼ green bell pepper, diced

¼ red bell pepper, diced

5 hard-boiled eggs, diced

1 to 2 tablespoons sweet salad cubes

⅓ cup regular or light mayonnaise

Half fill a medium stockpot with water and bring to a boil over high heat.

Add the salt and pepper, then add the shrimp and stir. Cook for 3 to 4 minutes, until the shrimp turn pink, then drain in a colander and set the shrimp aside to cool.

When the shrimp are cool, cut them in half, or smaller pieces—whatever size you like. Put them in a large serving bowl along with the onion, dill, pimento, celery, bell peppers, eggs, and sweet salad cubes. Stir in the mayonnaise and mix well. Taste and adjust the seasoning, then cover and refrigerate for 30 minutes to 1 hour before serving.

Marinade Shrimp, Tomato, and Onion Sallet

Serve this dish with a slotted spoon so the vinegar marinade drains back into the bowl. This salad also tastes great dressed with a light mayonnaise as a substitute for the vinegar and oil in the recipe.

Serves 4

1 teaspoon salt

1½ teaspoons pepper

1 pound medium-size raw shrimp, peeled and deveined

3 whole tomatoes, cut into wedges

1 purple onion, diced or thinly sliced

¼ white or red onion, cut into thin strips

¼ green bell pepper, cut into thin strips

¼ red bell pepper, cut into thin strips

¼ yellow bell pepper, cut into thin strips

½ teaspoon sugar

1 teaspoon minced garlic

1 cup vinegar (balsamic, distilled white, and red wine work equally well)

⅔ cup vegetable oil

Juice of 1 lemon

Half fill a medium stockpot with water and bring to a boil over high heat.

Add the salt and 1 teaspoon of the pepper, then add the shrimp and stir. Cook for 3 to 4 minutes, until the shrimp turn pink, then drain in a colander and set the shrimp aside to cool.

Put the cooled shrimp in a bowl along with the tomatoes, onion, bell peppers, the remaining ½ teaspoon pepper, the sugar, and garlic. Toss until well combined. Add the vinegar and oil and toss to coat. Cover and refrigerate for 35 to 45 minutes. Or eat right away!

Island Ways of Doin

Daufuskie is a small unique sea island surrounded by the Atlantic Ocean and one of several off the South Carolina shore. Unlike its neighbor Hilton Head, it is not connected with a bridge to the busy mainland. It's a place of beauty, peace, and tranquility far removed from the hectic pace going on morning, noon, and night elsewhere. Daufuskie can only be reached by boat from Hilton Head Island; Bluffton, South Carolina; or Savannah, Georgia. For this reason, changes have been slow to come to 'Fuskie and the Gullah community.

The Gullah who live on island have a long-standing practice of hunting, fishing, foraging, and growing a lot of what we eat. Since my childhood, there have been changes to our way of life, of course, but the foods we love have remained simple. Here are reflections on what I have seen change in my lifetime.

Transportation

Nowadays, people travel around the island mostly in golf carts. There are more trucks and cars, but not too many as of now. Most roads are not paved, and vehicles must be brought over by a barge. Getting some services on the island can take much longer than on the mainland. Being on island time is a much slower pace. It wasn't so long ago when we used wooden wagons pulled by an ox or a horse to get around the dirt roads of the community. The midwife who lived on the island used a horse-drawn carriage to do her work until 1969.

The durable wagon was used for hauling heavy loads and taking people places on the island they did not want to walk. It was inexpensive—and the ride was a little rugged sometime due to the state of the dirt roads—but dependable.

Naturally, because of their importance, we took especially good care of our animals.

Woodstoves and Wood Heaters

I was born at a time when wood-fired cooking stoves and heaters were all we had for cooking and keeping warm. We had to keep the cast-iron kitchen stove full of wood to provide a steady heat for cooking. These stoves became a thing of the past when they were replaced by propane-fueled stoves during the late 1970s and '80s. Wood heaters lasted until the late 1980s and early '90s, long after the wood kitchen stoves became obsolete, because our houses were not insulated and there was no other technology available to warm our homes.

Water, and Our Hand Pump

Electricity was not available until the early 1950s, so in order to get water for ourselves and our animals, we had to pump it by hand, pushing the handle of a hand pump back and forth until the water from underground flowed freely. Our hand pump was beyond our backyard under a big oak shade tree, and many gallons were pumped daily for cooking, drinking, cleaning, and bathing. And we pumped even more on wash day. Remember, this water all had to be hauled in buckets to wherever it was needed . . . and believe me, water weighs a lot! It was not until the 1970s that most hand pumps were replaced by electric pumps and water lines with spigots were finally installed in our kitchens.

Kerosene Lamps and Lights

When I was a child we used kerosene lamps to light our house at night. The light wasn't very bright, but we never knew the difference because we could see all that we needed at night. Every day before the sun went down, we had to clean the thin glass shades and refill each lamp with kerosene. We had one or two lamps in most rooms. We ate, bathed, studied, and listened to Momma and Pop or some neighbor telling stories by kerosene lamps. When we went to bed, all of the lamps were blown out to save kerosene for the next day.

Electricity

Electricity was brought to the island in 1953, but it took a while to spread. My grandmother and a few others had electricity because they could afford it, but many of us—like my parents—didn't get it until the mid-1960s when they could pay to have their house wired. And then they restricted our use of it because of the cost. We had to make sure no lights were on if no one was in that room; and if our parents were in bed, we could not sit up and talk with the lights on.

Telephone

Our communication between one another was face to face; we knew nothing about talking through the wires, and certainly nothing about the wireless communications we have today. But we never minded. Having neighbors come by to relate the news was a treat. Sometimes people stopped by to check in on one another and catch up on talking about their garden, hogs, or fishing stories. But when something was serious—like a death or a storm warning or church time—it was announced by the ringing of our church bell on the island. Word would travel from neighbor to neighbor so that everyone knew within a short time what the problem was.

The first telephones were installed during the 1970s when the owners of the phone company from Savannah decided that we Gullahs should have them. (Before that, the telephone company servicing the area decided that Daufuskie really did not need telephone lines because the company did not see a profit factor; most folks living there couldn't afford a phone.) Communication was no longer personal, one-on-one communication between the folks on the island, but extended across the water to family and friends. Folks slowly adjusted, but were not pleased with the new changes for a long time.

Down-Home Red Tada Sallet

This tada sallet can be made with the skin on or off. I like to leave the skin on, as red potatoes can get too mushy if you peel before boiling them. The skin is tender and adds a nice color.

Serves 6 to 8

8 to 10 large red potatoes, skin on, rinsed, and cut into bite-size pieces

1 teaspoon salt, or more to taste

1 teaspoon pepper, or more to taste

2 teaspoons minced garlic

½ onion, finely diced

5 to 6 hard-boiled eggs, diced

½ rib celery, diced

¼ red bell pepper, diced

¼ green bell pepper, diced

2 to 3 tablespoons sweet salad cubes

2 tablespoons hot sauce (optional)

1 teaspoon paprika

½ to ⅔ cup regular or light mayonnaise

Half fill a large pot with water and bring to a boil over medium-high heat, then add the potatoes. Season with the salt and pepper, then add 1 teaspoon of the garlic and half of the onion. Cook for 12 to 15 minutes, until the potatoes are tender but firm, not soft or mushy. As they cook, taste a piece several times to check for doneness. When done, drain well and put in a large serving bowl.

When the potatoes have just slightly cooled, add the eggs, celery, bell peppers, sweet salad cubes, the remaining garlic and onion, the hot sauce (if using), and paprika and toss to combine. Add the mayonnaise and gently stir to combine. Taste and adjust the seasonings if needed. Serve warm, or if you prefer, you can cover and refrigerate before serving—enjoy it the way you like it.

Simple Salmon Sallet

We used canned salmon to make this salad growing up, because we couldn't catch salmon on Daufuskie. I've made this recipe with fresh salmon. If you decide to use fresh fish, cook it lightly so that the flesh isn't firm, and it will flake easily.

Serves 6 to 8

2 tablespoons vegetable oil

1½ cups dried macaroni pasta

2 (3-ounce) cans wild salmon in water, drained

½ small white or red onion, finely diced

¼ green bell pepper, finely diced

¼ red bell pepper, finely diced

1 to 2 tablespoons sweet salad cubes

4 to 5 hard-boiled eggs, chopped

¼ to ½ cup regular or light mayonnaise

Half fill a stockpot with water, add the oil, and bring to a boil over high heat. Add the pasta and cook according to the package directions—until tender, but not mushy. Drain and let cool in a colander.

In a medium serving bowl, combine the salmon, onion, bell peppers, sweet salad cubes, and eggs. Add the macaroni and lightly toss together, then add the mayonnaise and gently stir to combine. Cover and refrigerate for 30 minutes to 1 hour before serving.

Lowcountry Crab and Macaroni Sallet

For a lighter version of this salad, you can substitute a vinaigrette or Italian dressing for the mayonnaise; omit the hard-boiled eggs, because an oil-based dressing will make them look too messy.

Serves 6 to 8

1½ cups dried macaroni pasta, cooked according to the package directions and cooled

2 cups lump crabmeat

1 teaspoon fresh or dried thyme

1 teaspoon pepper

1 teaspoon paprika

¼ green bell pepper, diced

¼ red bell pepper, diced

2 tablespoons sweet salad cubes

½ onion, diced

4 hard-boiled eggs, diced

¼ cup regular or light mayonnaise

Put the cooled macaroni in a large serving bowl and add the crabmeat, thyme, pepper, paprika, bell peppers, sweet salad cubes, onion, and eggs. Toss to combine, then gently stir in the mayonnaise. Cover and refrigerate for 30 minutes to 1 hour before serving.

Grandmomma

I sometimes envision my grandmomma Blossom as she stood bow-legged in her field, one hand holding on to her hoe, and wiping sweat from around her face with her handkerchief. She was ready to get busy with her day's work, heading out to her field real early so that she could get most of her chopping done before the sun got high and hot. She liked nothing more than spending countless hours planting and couldn't wait to chop the weeds from round her prize vegetables that were growing so well. I sometime daydream of her chopping weeds and humming an old folk song . . . thinking of nuttin specially, but getting finished so she can get started on getting something else done.

While her Indian and African genes made her look strong-willed, she had a kind and giving soul. She was always determined to finish whatever she started, and didn't settle for less when it didn't meet her liking. And she would remind us grandchurn that hard work will pay off if you stop thinking about not wanting to do it and just go ahead and get it done.

Grandmomma had good vision and she could see a long way off, but most time she would squint her eyes halfway closed as if she needed glasses. She always wore her dress well below her knees, with her homemade apron that had two big pockets on each side tied around her waist. There were certain things Grandmomma didn't tolerate, and she would be ready to let you know that she wasn't one to be mess with if yah needed ta know. Grandmomma especially didn't allow anyone to waste her time with foolishness. She had a way with words, and when she spoke, she was long-winded and would keep talking without stopping until she was finished. And after getting in her every word, she would let you know that she done said her piece, and that you had to decide what you were going to do, but in the meantime, just move outta her way.

Grandmomma never showed that she was tired of housework, planting, or doing all that she could to put good food on the table. Each year about a month before time to plant, she would sort through her seeds that were left from the crop of the year before, which she dried and put away for the next planting season.

Sometime before planting season, Grandmomma would pull out her almanac to check for the right moon phase and tide before planting certain vegetables. It was known that some vegetables wouldn't grow right or very little would bear when the moon or the tide wasn't right.

Grandmomma had a real love for all her vegetables, but she loved okra the most and made sure that she planted more of it than other vegetables, in a separate area where they grew best. She would say that her okra needed its own space to grow in order to bear a lot.

Beyond that, when all the planting, tending, and growing was done, and it came time for picking and gathering, Grandmomma didn't mind sharing with anyone who wanted some. She was generous with food—always willing to give a neighbor some vegetables from her garden. She usually cooked extra food just in case a hungry soul stumbled by. Many times the aroma from her slow-cooked meal would lead folks from the island's main road through a wooded path to her doorstep. She would smile when she saw them coming and didn't mind fixing them up a plate, piled high (she would, though, greet them at the gate so her chickens wouldn't get out and be lost in the woods).

"Comeyah and sit down at me table and get yah hungree belly fill wit me humney," she would say with a big smile on her face. "No need fo hunah chillen be hungree when da is food around. Now eat up, dares plenty mo in dah pot way dat one come from."

This sort of hospitality was not unusual on Daufuskie. Most folks who got to sit and eat at a native table on Daufuskie would be overwhelmed by the kindness a stranger from yondah would receive. No sooner they break bread than they were friends, and would be welcomed back in good faith. Kindness and manners were a part of family pride, and stood for the way you were brought up. Folks would never let us forget that manners and respect would carry you places money wouldn't in dissha world, but you had to use and show those manners to see how much difference they made.

Ova Dah Seafood Sallet

If you buy fresh lump crabmeat, make sure it has been picked. Fresh lump crabmeat is precooked, and so is canned lump crabmeat. The only time you need to cook the crabmeat for this recipe is if you use fresh crabs, which you need to boil before picking them.

Serves 8

1 teaspoon salt, or more to taste

1 teaspoon pepper, or more to taste

¼ pound medium-size raw shrimp, peeled and deveined

6 ounces cooked lump crabmeat (if you don't have any fresh picked crabmeat, pasteurized or canned lump crabmeat will do)

½ cup small tender conch, boiled and finely diced (available in spring and summer; ask at your local seafood market)

4 to 5 hard-boiled eggs, diced

½ rib celery, finely diced

¼ piece red bell pepper, diced

¼ piece green bell pepper, diced

½ small onion, finely diced

2 heaping tablespoons sweet salad cubes

1 teaspoon minced garlic

1 teaspoon mustard

1 teaspoon paprika

1 pinch dried thyme

⅔ cup regular or light mayonnaise, or to taste

Salt and pepper to taste

Lettuce leaves, for serving

Half fill a medium stockpot with water and bring to a boil over high heat.

Add the salt and pepper, then add the shrimp and stir. Cook for 3 to 4 minutes, until the shrimp turn pink, then drain in a colander and set the shrimp aside to cool.

In a large mixing bowl, toss together the shrimp, crabmeat, conch, eggs, celery, bell peppers, onion, sweet salad cubes, garlic, mustard, paprika, and thyme. Add the mayonnaise and mix well. Taste and add a pinch or two of salt and pepper for taste if needed. Cover and refrigerate for 30 minutes to 1 hour before serving.

Serve on a bed of lettuce.

Cucumber, Tomato, Raisin, and Purple Onion Sallet

We used to eat this salad only in the summer because that's when the cucumbers and tomatoes were ripe in our garden, but it's good anytime!

Serves 6 to 8

3 small or medium cucumbers, peeled or not, cut into medium coins

3 firm ripe tomatoes, stemmed and cut into wedges

1 purple or sweet onion, thinly sliced

½ cup dark raisins

½ cup vegetable oil or olive oil

½ cup red wine or distilled white vinegar

2 cloves garlic, crushed

1 teaspoon salt

½ teaspoon pepper

Put the cucumbers and tomatoes in a medium bowl. Add the onion, raisins, oil, vinegar, garlic, salt, and pepper. Use a large spoon to gently combine. Cover and refrigerate for 45 minutes to 1 hour before serving.

Drinkin, Talkin, and Momma's Home Remedies

I am so glad that my parents, grandparents, and neighbors loved me and took the time to share many of their life stories, ways, and beliefs with me and my siblings.

Today when I look back on my childhood, I realize those were my best years and I treasure them deeply. I never knew that we were poor because our way of life did not make us feel that we were. We didn't want change for better because there was nothing wrong with the way we were living and it didn't cost us what we did not have. So after I left the island, I decided to cling tighter to my ancestors' ways, to cherish them and do my best to pass on what they have taught me and the importance of their ways.

I recall the many times when folks would sit on their front porch, under one of the big old oak or mulberry trees that shaded our big backyard, and share many treasured memories. Those times gave me so much pride and love, knowing that folks had a heart for all, not just themselves.

Folks would laugh out loud while telling stories and sipping on some of their recently fermented homemade wine, or back-in-the-woods moonshine. Wine was made from fresh-picked blackberries, grapes, pears, persimmons, or plums that were gathered, placed in a container, and fermented under watchful eyes. No preservatives or chemicals were added—the wine was made from good natural fruit, love, and fermenting time.

Sometimes, after all the work was done, folks enjoyed sitting outside when a full moon was making the night bright and beautiful. My sisters and I were fascinated by many of their conversations, but we were only allowed to listen in on certain ones. If she felt the conversation was not for young ears, Momma would let us know that "dis is grown folks talk now, go find sumtin to do." We knew that we best do what she said and get stepping, not dragging our feet like we don't know what she was talking bout. As the conversation went on, accompanied by a few more drinks, their voices got louder. Between the talking and the drinking, and emptying and refilling the pint jars, their words would be more grown-up and more in Gullah language. By the time they were caught up with the news, gossip, and memories of yesteryear they knew they had tomorrow to look forward to, and they would say their goodbyes, and walk their neighbors partway home.

Momma and Pop were not book-smart, but they sure knew a lot about surviving and raising us to be good, mannered folks. Pop would preach to us that every day was a chance for a new start or to make things better. He had a lot of talent and didn't mind sharing it with us every chance he got. And for a man who didn't go to church, he knew a lot of sayings from the Bible.

He would remind us that God didn't make the world in one day, and he even took time to have a day of rest. Pop taught us that time should not be wasted on things that you cannot change or don't have any control over.

Staying at home and not going to school was not an option unless we were really sick and needed a doctor; otherwise we had to get up extra early to do our morning chores, and Momma and Pop made sure we got all the schooling that was being offered. They were not able to help us with most of our homework, but made sure that if we needed help we got it. At times Momma wanted to learn more about our homework and would sit at the table as we did our homework shortly after we got our chores done.

Every morning we had to make up our beds the minute we got out of them and leave our room clean, and we had to feed and care for our animals outside before walking through the woods to school.

Pop was a man who did not separate girls' work from the boys'; having us all do hard work helped build our muscles and our ability to do more as we get older. He felt having a man doing the toughest or heaviest work when needed was okay, but figured if you don't end up with a strong man, how are you going to survive if you are weak?

If one of us showed a sign of being a little bit sick, Momma could see it in our eyes and could tell if our sickness was fake or not. If she heard one of us sniffle or cough, Momma didn't waste any time but would get to work making her home remedies. She would grab her hoe, crooker (a burlap sack), and an axe or hatchet and rush off into the woods to gather the fixins for her remedy. She knew just where to go, and shortly after picking through bushes and different types of roots, she would return with them, smiling and ready to fix our ailments. She would first have us check it all for bugs, clean it, and break it all up for boiling in a big pot.

Momma always made sure that she brewed up enough of her home remedy so that everyone would get a good dose or two if needed, and sometimes she would even fix some for a neighbor if they needed some. By the time the home remedy had brewed, we would have eaten our supper, cleaned up, and bathed for bed. Right before going to bed she would have us line up, giving each one of us a tin cup almost full of the brew to drink. It tasted very bitter and yucky, but Momma and Pop would make sure we drank it all. We were sent off to bed to cover up so that we would sweat out our ailment before morning. Snuggling under one of her handmade quilts for the night helped make a restful sleep and, come morning, we were ready to join in and do our chores as Momma and Pop would want us to. Whatever it was she brewed up for us, it had a powerful punch that invariably cured us.

Keeping us busy and in line was one of Pop and Momma's most important accomplishments, and we never dared challenge them. Together, they raised ten kids (eight of us were girls), and they kept a close eye on each one of us.

Carrot, Raisin, and Pineapple Sallet

I like to use tidbit pineapple, which is smaller cuts of the fruit. The can will say "tidbit" on it. These smaller chunks work best with the grated carrots.

Serves 4 to 6

4 to 6 carrots, peeled and grated

⅔ cup dark raisins

1 (20-ounce) can pineapple tidbits (⅔ cup), drained

⅓ to ½ cup regular or light mayonnaise

Combine the carrots, raisins, pineapple, and mayonnaise in medium bowl, and mix together well. Cover and refrigerate for 30 minutes to 1 hour before serving.

Creamy Fresh Coleslaw

I love cabbage, whether it is cooked or served fresh in a delightful crisp sallet like this one.

Serves 4 to 6

Slaw:

½ small green cabbage, shredded

½ small red cabbage, shredded

2 large carrots, peeled and grated

½ sweet onion, thinly sliced

Homemade Dressing:

⅔ cup mayonnaise

½ cup sour cream

Salt and pepper to taste

¼ cup apple cider vinegar or distilled white vinegar

1 teaspoon garlic powder

Make the slaw: In a large bowl, toss together the cabbages, carrots, and onion.

Make the dressing: In a small bowl, whisk together the mayonnaise, sour cream, a pinch each of salt and pepper, the vinegar, and garlic until well combined. Taste to correct the seasoning.

Drizzle the dressing slowly over the slaw, and toss well to combine. Cover and refrigerate for 30 minutes to 1 hour before serving.

Cranberry Turkey Sallet

It don't have to be Thanksgiving to eat turkey. Just sayin.

Serves 6 to 8

1½ pounds cooked deboned turkey, both white and dark meat

Salt and pepper to taste

5 to 6 hard-boiled eggs, diced

½ rib celery, diced

½ cup diced red bell pepper

½ cup diced green bell pepper

1 cup pecan pieces

⅓ to ½ cup dried cranberries

½ teaspoon fresh or dried thyme

¼ to ½ cup regular or light mayonnaise

4 to 5 lettuce leaves, for serving

2 tomatoes, stemmed and cut into wedges

Chop the turkey meat into bite-size pieces and put in a medium bowl. Sprinkle with salt and pepper and toss. Add the eggs, celery, bell peppers, pecans, and cranberries and toss well. Add the thyme and mayonnaise and toss lightly.

Line a platter or bowl with lettuce, add the salad, and arrange the tomato wedges on top. Cover and refrigerate for 30 minutes to 1 hour before serving.

One Hand Wash dah Other

Granddaddy wasn't a big man, but he lived a full life until he was ninety-six years old. Even to his end, I never heard him complain about anything. He felt that being ready to die was a part of living a full life. He loved my grandmomma with all his heart and always spoke highly of her.

He was a man of very few words when it came to talking. He loved spending time out of the house and, like most men back then, he believed housework was women's work. When he wasn't busy doing chores, he would gather his bucket and fishing needs and head off to the dock or creek to catch a few fresh fish for dinna. He also enjoyed hunting, crabbing, picking oysters, and digging for clams.

There was a time, before the changes came to the island, when he and others would find a spot deep in the woods and brew up gallons of moonshine (white lightning). Even though moonshine was illegal to make, folks did it anyway. Being a peaceful soul, Granddaddy was loved by all and would give you the shirt off his back if he knew you needed it more.

I got much joy listening to Granddaddy telling us about his childhood days. He would tell us how, when the tide was low, folks could once walk from Daufuskie across the Calibogue Sound to Hilton Head Island before it was dredged out.

The two islands—Daufuskie and Hilton Head—were much alike back in the day. At one time, folks on Hilton Head also needed a boat to get off the island for their needs.

Granddaddy saw how things had changed from when he was young, and how things were still changing because folks wanted more and more for less. He realized that was not all bad, but with all the rushing folks was doing, they were losing a lot of self-respect, and had no time to care about others. He used to say that keeping your hands balled up in a fist meant you can't give or receive anything in them. Like other folks, Granddaddy also felt that one hand wash dah other. When you help someone, someone help you.

To us, it seemed impossible that at one time a thousand or more folks lived on Daufuskie. But it was true, and many of us kids played in those old abandoned houses. Living on Daufuskie was best when school was out and our cousins from the big city across the water—Savannah—came to visit. Their parents would send them shortly after school closed to spend the summer in the country, where they believed it would be safer to play. And once they got on the island we couldn't wait to get together and play. Sometime they would teach us new games and things that we had not heard of on our little island.

We often would head to Grandmomma and Granddaddy's house where the cousins stayed, or they would come and help us with our chores so we could finish faster. Watching television was not a part of our enjoyment, even though Grandmomma was one of few who had a television set at the time. We had fun playing house and gathering things from the garden, pretending to be adults and cooking like they did. Some days we would simply run through the woods from one end of the island to the other.

Pecan Daufuskie Chicken Sallet

Whether using a fresh-cooked chicken or leftovers, this recipe makes a great side sallet for six people, or the main meal for four.

Serves 4 to 6

½ pound white chicken meat, baked or boiled

½ pound dark chicken meat, baked or boiled

¼ green bell pepper, finely diced

¼ red bell pepper, finely diced

½ rib celery, finely diced

1 teaspoon garlic powder

3 tablespoons sweet salad cubes

2 teaspoons paprika

1 teaspoon black or white pepper

4 hard-boiled eggs, diced

⅓ to ½ cup pecan pieces

2 to 3 heaping tablespoons mayonnaise

Chop the chicken meat and put in a bowl with the bell peppers, celery, garlic powder, sweet salad cubes, paprika, black or white pepper, and eggs. Toss well, then add the pecans and mayonnaise and toss well again. Cover and refrigerate for 30 minutes to 1 hour before serving.

Easy Egg Sallet

This is great on toast or as a sandwich. Or just enjoy it as a snack on crackers.

Serves 4

6 hard-boiled medium eggs, diced

1 teaspoon pepper

1 tablespoon sweet pickle relish or sweet salad cubes

½ teaspoon garlic powder

2 dashes hot sauce

1 pinch salt

Mayonnaise, as much or little as desired

Put the eggs in a bowl, along with the pepper, relish, garlic powder, hot sauce, salt, and mayonnaise. Toss well to combine, then taste and correct the seasoning if needed. Cover and refrigerate for 30 minutes to 1 hour before serving.

Dah Birds

Chicken, Duck, and Turkey All dah Way

I remember my childhood as being filled with chores. The first one in the day was getting up extra early in the morning to care for our livestock. We didn't get to take a day off, or feed the animals at a later time, no matter what the weather was gonna do. And during the warmer summer months we had to make sure that all the animals and birds had plenty of fresh water at all time. Sometime when the weather was hot the birds would take a bath, splashing in their pail of drinking water to help stay cool; it was fun to watch them as they fluttered and flapped their wings, spreading the water all over themself. When the chicken grew feathers sometime they would get smart and climb up on the highest nesting area and fly over the fence. Momma could see that it was time to clip their wings to keep them safe in their fenced yard.

Before leaving Daufuskie to further my education I thought everyone raised their own livestock for their meals, as we did, until I witnessed folks in the city and on the mainland depending on grocery stores for most of their needs. Those folks did not get the joy of knowing how and what their animals ate, or watching them grow and mature, changing their colors and size from babies to adult—an experience all by itself.

Island Pineapple and Coconut Chicken

Everybody loves a baked chicken. I like the sweet, crunchy taste the pineapple and coconut add to the meat in this dish.

Serves 4

1 (3- to 5-pound) whole chicken, cleaned

1 to 2 teaspoons salt

1 teaspoon pepper

2 (11.5-ounce) cans frozen pineapple juice concentrate, thawed

1½ cups fresh pineapple, diced

½ cup unsweetened dried coconut

Preheat the oven to 365°F.

Pat the chicken dry and place in a large roasting pan.

Combine the salt and pepper together in a little bowl, and sprinkle over all the chicken. Rub a dash or two inside the cavity.

Pour the pineapple juice concentrate into the pan around the chicken, and add 1 cup of the fresh pineapple to the pan. Place the remaining ½ cup pineapple inside the chicken cavity.

Sprinkle the coconut over the chicken, cover the pan with a lid or aluminum foil, and place in the center of the oven. Roast for 1½ hours, then remove the cover and use a long-handled spoon to baste the chicken well all over and inside the cavity. Cover the pan again and cook for 1 hour more. Remove from the oven and check for doneness. When a fork is inserted into the meat, the juices should run clear. If needed, baste again, place the uncovered pan back in the oven, and bake for 10 minutes, or until the skin is slightly brown. Remove from the oven, carve, and serve hot.

(Oh My Goodness) Orange Chicken

If you like the citrus taste of orange with chicken, you will enjoy the baked orange slices, too.

Serves 4

1 (3- to 5-pound) chicken, cleaned

2 teaspoons salt

2 teaspoons pepper

1 teaspoon minced fresh garlic or garlic powder

2 (5.5-ounce) cans frozen orange juice concentrate, thawed

1 orange, sliced medium-thick, peeled or unpeeled

Preheat the oven to 360°F.

Place the chicken in a large roaster pan.

Combine the salt, pepper, and garlic in a small bowl, and sprinkle or pat the seasoning all over the chicken and inside the cavity. Pour three-quarters of the orange juice into the pan around the chicken, and pour the remaining juice inside the cavity.

Place the orange slices around the chicken and tuck a few inside the cavity. Cover with a lid or aluminum foil and roast for 2 to 2½ hours. Remove the cover and use a long-handled spoon to baste the chicken every 15 minutes for 45 minutes, or until brown on top. Carve and serve.

Mango Chicken

I never had a mango growing up on Daufuskie Island, but once I tasted them as an adult, I found ways to add them to recipes. Here, it adds a lot of flavor to the chicken. It's a great dish to make when mangoes are in season!

Serves 4

1 (3- to 5-pound) chicken, cleaned and cut into pieces

1 tablespoon salt

1 tablespoon pepper

4 ripe mangoes, peeled, pitted, and cut into pieces

Preheat the oven to 365°F.

Pour 1 cup water into a roasting pan, then arrange the chicken pieces in the pan so they don't overlap. Season with salt and pepper, then arrange the mango slices on top of the chicken. Cover the pan with a lid or aluminum foil and bake for 1½ hours, then remove the cover, baste the chicken, and bake uncovered for another 10 to 12 minutes, until the chicken is browned. Serve.

Gullah Chicken Gumbo

Some folks put okra in the pot without frying it, but I like to fry it first because it is less slimy and adds better texture to the gumbo.

Serves 6 to 8

1½ cups vegetable oil

1 onion, diced

½ large green bell pepper, diced

½ large red bell pepper, diced

10 to 12 tomatoes, diced

½ (6-ounce) can tomato paste

1 tablespoon salt

1 tablespoon pepper

1 teaspoon chopped fresh basil

1 teaspoon dried or fresh thyme leaves

1½ pounds white and dark meat chicken
    pieces, bone in, skin on

1½ to 2 pounds okra, cut into 1-inch rounds

Rice, biscuits, or cornbread, for serving

In a large stockpot, heat ½ cup of the oil over medium-high heat, then stir in the onion and bell peppers and fry for 3 minutes. Add the tomatoes, tomato paste, salt, pepper, basil, thyme, and 1½ quarts water. Bring to a boil over medium-high heat, then cover the pot, lower the heat to medium-low, and simmer for 45 minutes, stirring on occasion.

Taste to check the seasoning, than add the chicken and cook for 35 to 45 minutes, stirring on occasion, until the chicken is fork tender, but not falling from the bone. Set aside.

Heat the remaining 1 cup oil in a 12-inch skillet over medium-high heat, then add the okra and fry for 4 to 5 minutes, turning, until it begins to brown. Remove with a slotted spoon and drain on paper towels.

Add the fried okra to the gumbo pot and cook for another 20 to 30 minutes. Serve hot with your choice of rice, biscuits, or cornbread.

Birds of a Feather

During the spring months the chickens, ducks, and turkeys would mate and soon start laying their eggs. Little ducklings are so cute, and they have a walk of their own: they wobble. They can swim from the time they are born and, like most babies, stay close to their mother until they're grown.

Duck eggs are bigger than chicken or turkey eggs. Momma would keep a close eye on all the birds when they started laying, for several reasons. Each day Momma would have us gather and separate the eggs from the chickens, ducks, or turkeys. Some eggs was for eating and others were collected in a bowl, covered, and placed in a cool safe place. After collecting enough and when the hens stopped laying, it would be time to place several dozen eggs in each nest for the chickens, ducks, or turkeys that was ready to set on the eggs long enough to have bitties (small chicks), poults (small turkeys), or ducklings.

When this time came for the hens to set, Momma would gather their eggs from the bowl and mark (scratch) the eggs lightly with a sharp pencil. This would let her know that the eggs in the nest were for hatching, in case a laying hen got on the nest and laid a fresh new egg while the setting hen was off taking a bite to eat. Marking the eggs was a reminder, and a smart way to keep up with the hens. She would then place the marked eggs under the chickens, ducks, or turkeys that were ready to set.

Mom made sure we checked all the nests every day. She would then mark her calendar from the time she set her chickens to a period of about twenty-one days, on a full moon.

When the sound of baby chicks hatching was heard from under the hen, my momma would gather each egg that had cracked and place the chicks in a box until all had hatched. This protected them from getting knocked out of the nest, or eaten by snakes. When all the eggs were hatched (sometime a few would not), Momma would place the small chicks in a separate coop with their mother, who would take over and keep the little ones safe from that point.

Keeping the babies with their mother in a separate area shortly after hatching was to protect them from any creatures that wanted to eat them. Each mother bird would keep her babies close, and at any sign of danger they had a special call for the babies to come close for protection. The hen would open up her wings so that her babies would all gather under them to be safe.

Turkeys require a little more care to raise because they are more sensitive about what they can eat as babies. I remember Momma would have us collect a type of weed that grew two to three feet high near our yard. (We called it Juliesmoke, but I still don't know what the actual name is.) She would show us how to chop it up real fine, squeeze the juice out from it with a cloth, let it dry, and then feed it to the baby turkeys. They could digest it better than corn or grits. Small chicks, ducks, and turkeys could not eat the whole corn we fed the adults because the kernels were too big for them to swallow. We could not give them raw grits because it would swell in their craw, making them unable to breathe and killing them in a short time.

Raising animals was interesting, and watching them grow and feed on different things as they got bigger taught me a lot about their life cycle and their markings and "duties."

A male chicken is called a rooster, and he would crow mostly early morning when the sun was rising (some would say he was the barnyard pimp!). A rooster is identified by its high, fluffy back tail, the larger crown on its head, and a sharp spur on the back of each foot. The hens have a small crown and no spurs. A chicken can lay eggs without mating with a rooster, but the eggs will not hatch.

A full-grown male turkey is called a tom or a gobbler and he spreads his wings, making a clucking sound as he prances and dragging his feathers against the ground to show how big and pretty he is. A female turkey is called a hen, a young male turkey is called a jake, and baby turkeys are called poults or chicks. A group of domesticated turkeys is commonly called a rafter.

Southern Smuttered Fried Chicken

The addition of gravy to classic fried chicken add another layer of flavor and tenderness that you'll love. This is a crowd-pleaser.

Serves 4

2 to 3 cups vegetable oil

1 (3- to 5-pound) chicken, cleaned and cut into pieces

2 tablespoons salt, plus more to taste

2 tablespoons pepper, plus more to taste

2 tablespoons garlic powder

2 tablespoons paprika

2 cups self-rising flour

1 onion, chopped

¼ green bell pepper, chopped

½ red bell pepper, chopped

½ rib celery, diced

3 cups hot water, or just enough to barely cover the chicken

In a large skillet, heat the oil over medium-high heat until hot but not smoking. Toss the chicken pieces with a combination of the salt, pepper, garlic powder, and paprika. Put the flour in a bag (or bowl), and add the chicken, 3 or 4 pieces at a time, tossing to coat with the flour.

Shake excess flour off each piece of chicken and use tongs to slide it carefully into the hot oil, working in batches so you do not crowd the skillet. Cook for 2 to 4 minutes on each side, or until browned on each side (the chicken won't be cooked through yet). Carefully remove the chicken pieces from the oil and drain on paper towels.

When all the chicken pieces are browned, carefully pour the oil from the skillet, and place the pieces of chicken back in the skillet. Add the onion, bell peppers, and celery. Add hot water to cover the chicken, season with salt and pepper, and cover the skillet, leaving the lid slightly ajar. Cook over medium heat for 45 minutes, stirring occasionally, until the water thickens into gravy. Taste for seasoning. Turn the heat to very low to keep warm until you are ready to serve.

Country Stew Chicken with Vegetables

This is dinner in a bowl. Fresh vegetables and chicken—it's like a chicken pot pie but without the hassle of making the dough. Who doesn't love that?

Serves 6

½ cup vegetable oil

1 (3- to 5-pound) chicken, cleaned, cut into pieces, and patted dry

1 sweet onion, diced

1 rib celery, diced

1 tablespoon salt

2 teaspoons pepper

3 cups chicken stock or water, or more if needed

½ cup shelled sweet peas, fresh or frozen

½ cup whole fresh corn kernels cut from the cob

In a large stockpot, heat the oil over medium-high heat. Working in batches so you don't crowd the pot, add the chicken pieces, being careful not to splatter the oil. Fry for 4 to 6 minutes, until the pieces start to brown, then flip and fry for another 3 to 4 minutes until slightly browned. Add the onion, celery, salt, pepper, stock, peas, and corn. Stir for 1 to 2 minutes, cover, and cook over medium heat for 45 minutes to 1 hour, stirring on occasion. If needed, add ½ to 1 cup more stock or hot water, stirring up all the browned bits, so that the chicken don't stick to the pan. Check to see if the chicken is tender, correct the seasoning, and continue cooking for 20 to 30 minutes, until the meat is almost falling off the bones and the gravy has thickened. Once the chicken is done, decrease the heat to low and keep warm until ready to serve.

Before you serve, remove the chicken bones and skin and use two forks to shred the chicken meat.

Remembering the Last Native Island Country Store

In the 1920s through the 1950s there were several grocery stores on the island, but by the time I came along in the late '50s there was only one store left. I grew up hearing folks talk about those stores of long ago, mom-and-pop groceries where natives could trade for things they needed with something from dah gardens, or fresh chicken eggs from dah henhouse.

There were also two oyster factories and a lumber company that used to haul wood on a railroad track from one end of the island to the other. But during my younger days, those disappeared too. Gone . . . Only the memories and a few broken-down buildings are left from those yondah time.

Back in dah day, when Daufuskie had only one native store owner left in business, fo us it was like going to a big grocery store, even though compared to those on the mainland the choices were very limited. But we were happy with what we had, because living off the land was what we folks knew best and we made it meet our needs.

Our main grocery shopping was done in our backyard or in our fields, where we raised collards, corn, beans, peas, onions, potatoes, and tomatoes. We raised our own chickens, ducks, and turkeys, hogs, and cows. And we enjoyed a variety of wild game from the woods, like deer, rabbits, squirrels, and raccoons. There were lots of fruit, berry, and nut trees all around us.

We had more than enough fresh seafood year-round, including shrimp, fish, crabs, oysters, and clams, which we harvested from the ocean and creeks. The only time our folks had to go shopping on the mainland was for basic items like salt, pepper, sugar, rice and grits, tools, hardware, and now and then a piece of furniture.

My grandfather once said that, although he couldn't speak for other places, if you lived on Daufuskie and starved, you were a poor soul who was just lazy (or, put another way, a poor mole with one hole). We had all we needed for the life that we were born into. Daufuskie life challenged us in many ways, but we got through fine.

That last grocery store on the island was owned by a couple named Samuel and Blossom Holmes. They were both Daufuskie-born and loved the island as much as everyone else. And my memories of their little country store stay with me today because it was a fun place for us kids to spend a nickel or dime for some special treat. No matter if we'd been working or playing all day, we didn't mind walking a couple of miles from one end of the island to the other to get there.

I still remember the way the old wooden store smelled of cured and smoked meat, whether it be ham or smoke fish, hanging from a rope overhead in a corner. It made you feel like you were in a special place—and you were. There were things you could get if you couldn't wait to go to the mainland to shop—you could buy soda pop, can goods, or smoke bacon in the store. You could also find kerosene for lamps, turpentine, soap, clothespins and wire for clotheslines, wash tubs, foot tubs, hammers, nails, even small pieces of lumber. Of course, what we were interested in were the big half-full candy jars that sat on the counter, and the delicious johnnycake cookies (soft, light cookies about two inches across that went well with a soda pop). The little country store was a child's dream place, with sweets that we were only allowed to have every so often.

Mr. Holmes was a man with many talents. In addition to being a store owner, he was one of several great carpenters who built houses and the Mount Carmel church on Daufuskie. He also loved to hunt and go to the river to fish and crab. His wife, called Miz Blossom, had long ago been a midwife when she could be of help. She loved to garden, and raised her own chickens. My grandmother was also called Blossom, and to keep them apart, folks used to call Miz Holmes "Little Blossom" and my grandmother "Big Blossom" because of their relative sizes.

Their little country store didn't open or close on a set schedule; most time it was come and be served. Sometimes if the store was closed and you needed something, all you had to do was go to their house at a reasonable time of day and knock on their door. I could remember times when we would arrive at their home and Miz Holmes would be in her backyard scrubbing clothes on a washboard in a tub, while going back and forth to her kitchen to cook a meal. Waiting for her to break away and open the store for folks gave the grownups time to chat and catch up on the latest news. But for us kids, we knew we had to be patient and it would all be worth it.

As kids, we loved nothing more than to volunteer to go to the store for our parents; or if a neighbor wanted something but didn't feel like the walk or hitching up the cow to the wagon, they knew us kids didn't mind doing it for a chance to get away from home and the work. Depending on how long we had before getting back, we would stop by a friend's house and invite them to make the long walk with us. We would play games, sometime singing at the top of our lungs, or racing down the long dirt road to and from the store. Momma and Pop didn't mind us going as long as we didn't tarry too long, because there was always work at home to be done.

Sometime we were given a quarter to buy a treat. A quarter was big bucks for us kids. For that, we could buy a bag of cookies and a sixteen-ounce Nehi soda pop. We were limited on how much sweet stuff we could buy, because Miz Holmes knew all of our parents. Plus we all knew to save some of our money for other needs and not spend all of it in the store.

After the passing of Mr. Holmes, Miz Holmes was unable to keep up the stock in the store because she couldn't drive a boat and go back and forth to the mainland for supplies—and keep up with her housework, too. So the stock got lower and lower, and Miz Holmes finally closed the store.

We missed the last country store, but it wasn't long before changes came and there was a ferry boat to take us to the mainland more often. Most native folks then did their big shopping once a month, and we all helped each other out if we were going and a neighbor needed something. And when I became the oldest child at home Mom would sometime write her shopping list and send me over to Savannah or Bluffton on the monthly run to do the shopping for her. She knew that one day soon I would be leaving home for a higher education, and would be shopping for a family myself.

Honey Fried (or Baked) Chicken

This recipe tastes great either way, so I've provided directions for both frying and baking. The textures are different, but the honey is a winning addition to both versions.

Serves 4

1 (3- to 5-pound) chicken, cleaned, patted dry, and cut into pieces

2 to 2½ cups vegetable oil, if frying

1 tablespoon salt

2 teaspoons pepper

3 teaspoons garlic powder

1 tablespoon paprika

2 cups self-rising flour

½ to 1 cup warm honey

FRIED

In a 12-inch skillet, heat the oil over medium-high heat.

Combine the salt, pepper, garlic powder, and paprika in a small bowl.

Put the flour in a plastic bag (or bowl). Combine the seasoning with the flour and shake or stir together well.

Line a platter with paper towels.

Dredge 3 or 4 pieces of chicken at a time in the seasoned flour to coat well. Remove one piece at a time, and shake off any excess flour. Place the 3 or 4 pieces in the heated oil and fry for at least 5 minutes on each side, and longer for larger pieces, adjusting the heat if the chicken is browning too quickly, until browned and cooked through. Use a long-handled fork or tongs to transfer the chicken pieces to drain on the paper towel–lined platter. Repeat the process until all the chicken is fried.

Arrange the drained chicken on a platter and drizzle with honey. Serve hot.

BAKED

Preheat the oven to 375°F.

Place the chicken pieces in a baking pan large enough to fit all the pieces in one layer.

Combine the salt, pepper, garlic powder, and paprika in a small bowl. Sprinkle the seasoning over both sides of the chicken. Cover the pan with aluminum foil and bake for 1 to 1½ hours, until the chicken is fork tender.

Drain the chicken pieces on paper towels, arrange on a platter, and drizzle with a little honey—or a lot, if you like!

Bake 'Em Duck

We had plenty of duck growing up, because Momma loved to have them around the yard. When we ate them for special Sunday dinners or a holiday, it was the kids' job to choose one from the yard and pluck it. (Momma killed the duck, because I didn't like that part.) You had to dunk the bird in hot water to loosen the feathers, then hold it over a bucket to catch the feathers as you plucked. It took a good 30 minutes to pluck the whole bird, then we held it over a hot fire to singe the fine feathers so they'd fall off. Then it was ready for Momma to prepare it for cooking.

Serves 4

2 teaspoons salt

2 teaspoons pepper

1 tablespoon garlic powder

2 teaspoons dried or chopped fresh sage

2 teaspoons fresh or dried thyme

1 (5-pound, or more) whole duck, plucked and cleaned

Preheat the oven to 355°F.

Combine the salt, pepper, garlic powder, sage, and thyme in a small bowl. Sprinkle the mixture evenly all over the duck, with a little in the cavity.

Place the duck on a rack fitted in a roasting pan, cover with a lid or aluminum foil, and roast for 2 to 3 hours, until fork tender (the time will vary depending on the size of duck). When done, remove the cover and bake for 10 to 15 minutes longer, until the duck is lightly browned. Carve and serve.

Stew Duck

Cooking duck pieces on the stovetop is a quicker way to achieve tender meat—the consistent heat cuts the time almost in half.

Serves 4

¼ cup vegetable oil

1 (3- to 5-pound) whole duck, cleaned and cut into pieces

1 large sweet onion, diced

½ red bell pepper, diced

Salt and pepper to taste

Pat the duck pieces dry. Heat the oil in a large pot over high heat, and fry the duck pieces 3 or 4 at a time so as not to crowd the pot, for 3 to 4 minutes on each side.

Add the onion, bell pepper, salt and pepper, and enough water to cover the duck and cook, covered, over medium-high heat for 1½ hours, or until fork tender. Check at intervals for tenderness during the cooking, and when the duck pieces are tender, reduce the heat to medium and add a little more water and seasoning as needed. The cooking liquid will cook down so it is just covering the duck pieces.

Serve the duck pieces with the pan sauce.

Pineapple Orange Daufuskie Duck

Not only does the pineapple flavor the duck, but it also makes a great side dish to serve with it.

Serves 4

2 teaspoons salt

2 teaspoons pepper

1 (3- to 5-pound) whole duck, plucked and cleaned

3 to 4 cups pineapple chunks, fresh or canned

2 cups frozen orange juice concentrate, thawed

Preheat the oven to 355°F.

Combine the salt and pepper in a small bowl. Sprinkle the mixture evenly all over the duck.

Place the seasoned duck on a rack in a roasting pan, add the pineapple chunks around the bird, and tuck some in the cavity. Pour the orange juice concentrate around the duck, not over it, so that the seasoning stays on top. Cover with a lid or aluminum foil and roast for 1½ to 2 hours.

Uncover and baste the duck with orange juice from the pan several times, re-cover, and roast for 1 hour. Baste again and return, uncovered, to the oven for 10 to 15 minutes to brown.

Carve the duck and serve with the pineapple from the pan.

My Teacher, and One Unforgettable School Year

The year was 1969, and after a long hot summer on the island it was time to return to school. School was a welcome break from the many daily chores we had at home, and I was starting sixth grade. We didn't know this year would be different. Miss Frances Jones, who taught grades 1 through 4, had retired after teaching for thirty-five years at Mary Field School on Daufuskie. The one teacher who was left, Miss Julia Johnson, had previously taught grades 5 through 8, but she would now teach the younger students.

After arriving at our two-room schoolhouse, the eighteen of us in the older grades sat at our desks waiting. We did not have a clue who our new teacher would be—or how our education was about to change! We were trying to be quiet, because Miss Johnson was next door with the younger students, and she was checking on us to make sure we didn't misbehave; we'd had her the year before and knew she was tough as nails.

When the door opened, our eyes popped as a young white male with sideburns entered the classroom in a very upbeat way. He was far from what we expected—he didn't look like no teacher we'd had before. We sat speechless as he introduced himself. He first wrote his name on the blackboard in bold letters: PAT CONROY. Pat saw the looks on our faces and did not waste any time asking us our names. He then spent the next few hours meeting and greeting us, one by one. He also did something that no teacher had ever done for us before. He told us that he was not going to go by our past grades; he was going

to wipe the slate clean and give each one of us an A. All we had to do was work hard to keep it. We liked him a lot already. By the end of the day it was as if we was going to have a different kinda school year.

At first, Pat did not stay on the island like most teachers did. He lived on the mainland with his family and was given a boat so he could come and go as needed. He took time with us and went beyond teaching from the old textbook. He found an old projector and showed us movies on history and anything else that he could use to help us learn. Pat saw things wasn't right with the way we were being educated on island; he was even concerned about the milk we were drinking. At that time, we were still drinking powder milk for lunch instead of fresh milk in the little carton. He asked his supervisor why we weren't getting the fresh milk we needed and was told they could not get the milk to us without spoiling. Pat figured he had a boat and was coming over daily, so he began to bring the milk over himself.

Each day Pat made learning fun as he challenged our minds. Sometime he would invite friends who were musicians, photographers, or anyone who could be helpful to our education. Pat wanted us to have a broader understanding of what we would face once we left our island, so he decided we needed to get away and see some of the world "across the water." Even though most of our parents couldn't afford to send us on these trips, Pat made sure we all went on his dime. He escorted us to Washington, DC, for nearly a week and to Savannah for a day trip to a TV station. Pat's concern, passion, and vision in teaching us was real and heartfelt. He knew our situation was different, living on a bridgeless island, but he felt we deserved to learn—and could learn!—just as much as any other schoolkid on the mainland.

Pat Conroy believed that no matter where you are from or the color of your skin, you had the right to a good education.

After that year it was sad to see him go, and learning was never the same for me. Pat and I were not in touch again until he sent me a letter in September 1976, a year after I had graduated. The letter was an apology about being a little late in sending me one thousand dollars and included a check for that amount a few months later. You see, he wrote a book, *The Water Is Wide*, about his one year of teaching us on Daufuskie, that eventually became a movie called *Conrack*. He had told us he was writing a book about us and if it sold, he would make sure each of us kids got a thousand dollars, because we were in it. We really never believed it would happen, but at some point, everyone did get their thousand-dollar check from him.

Half-Stew, Half-Bake Duck

Duck is a tough bird, so you need to cook at a lower heat and for a longer time. It's never right when I try to cook it faster. The preparation for this dish is easy, it's just the cooking time that's long. I suggest you start this recipe about 5 hours before you expect to serve it.

Serves 4

1 (3- to 5-pound) whole duck, plucked, cleaned, and cut into pieces like a chicken (or ask your butcher to do that for you)

3 teaspoons salt

2 teaspoons pepper

3 teaspoons garlic powder

½ cup vegetable oil

1 large sweet onion, diced

1 rib celery, diced

In a small bowl, combine 2 teaspoons of the salt, 1 teaspoon of the pepper, and the garlic powder and sprinkle or pat all over the duck pieces.

In a medium stockpot, heat the oil over medium-high heat, then add the seasoned duck pieces and fry for 4 to 6 minutes on each side, until lightly browned. Remove to paper towels to drain.

Pour the remaining oil from the pot and return the duck to the pot over medium-high heat. Add the onion and celery, and enough water to come halfway up the sides of the pot. Stir in the remaining 1 teaspoon salt and 1 teaspoon pepper, cover, and cook for 2 hours, stirring on occasion.

Preheat the oven to 355°F.

Transfer the duck to a roasting pan with the juice and vegetables, cover, and bake for 1½ to 2 hours, until the duck is fork tender.

Spoon some of the sauce over the duck as you serve it.

Cranberry Bake Duck

This is a perfect holiday dish. The taste of the duck is richer and gamier than turkey. If you don't have many guests for the holiday, this is a wonderful alternative to the usual big bird. Another plus is that there are usually no leftovers!

Serves 4

1 (16-ounce) bag fresh cranberries

6 cups chicken broth

1 (3- to 5-pound) whole duck, plucked and cleaned

2 teaspoons salt

2 teaspoons pepper

Rinse the cranberries and place them in a medium saucepan over medium heat. Add the broth and cook for 15 minutes, or until the cranberries have broken down and the mixture has thickened. It will be chunky. Set aside to cool slightly.

Preheat the oven to 355°F.

In a small bowl, combine the salt and pepper and sprinkle or pat all over the duck and in the cavity. Place the duck in a roasting pan and pour the cranberry sauce around it. Cover with a lid or aluminum foil and roast for 2 hours, then baste well overall with the cranberry sauce in the pan. Cover, return the pan to the oven, and continue to roast for 45 minutes to 1 hour, basting occasionally, until the meat is fork tender. Uncover and roast for 20 to 35 minutes more, until browned.

Either eat the cranberry sauce on the side, or spoon it over the servings of duck.

Duck Stuffed with Oyster Rice

1 (3- to 5-pound) whole duck, cleaned
  and patted dry

1 teaspoon salt

1 teaspoon black pepper

1 teaspoon garlic powder

Gullah Oyster Rice, prepared without
  shrimp (page 137)

Preheat the oven to 360°F.

Place the duck in a roasting pan and season all over with the salt, pepper, and garlic powder. Roast, uncovered, for 1½ hours, then remove from the oven and baste with the juices in the pan. Return to the oven and roast for another 1 to 1½ hours, checking for doneness after 1 hour. When a meat thermometer inserted in the thickest part of the breast reads 165°F, the duck is done.

When you are ready to serve, place the duck on a platter. Stuff and surround the duck with oyster rice and serve immediately.

Pat Conroy's Voodoo Science

Pat Conroy initially did not have a clue what he was about to take on as a teacher on Daufuskie. And for our part, we did not know how much he would bring to our lives as our teacher. As the first weeks of the school year passed, Pat saw that we needed more than just reading, writing, and arithmetic from books that were old and outdated, so he showed us how to learn and have fun at the same time. Pat would make each day an adventure by giving us new challenges every day; he saw that we were learning a lot more and faster.

When he saw that we were restless, he would call on someone to tell a story about anything that was happening or going on with them. After months of telling him our stories, we realized that Pat liked the voodoo stories best—old hand-me-down tales that scared us as kids and kept us awake at night. Being a child and always listening to what was being said, sometimes you heard voodoo being vaguely mentioned: stories about something strange done to someone, like stealing some of their hair while they were sleeping and then using it in a ceremony to make them go crazy. I try not to believe in the dark side even though I have heard and seen some strange things in my time.

Like how once, when I was about eight years old, we thought a lady on the island was a witch. She wore black all the time: very witchy to us. When Momma sent us to her house on some errand, her dirt yard would be raked and there would be *no* footprints in the dirt that she raked. That scared us a lot.

There was a commonly whispered story about a woman who supposedly practiced voodoo who had gotten mad at her son. Soon he was bent over in terrible pain and rushed to the hospital on the mainland to be operated on. And what did they find that was causing the pain? *Snake eggs* in his abdomen.

Growing up I did not know and had never heard of the color "haint blue." A color some folks simply liked. Others had dah reason to believe it would keep away evil spirits. (*Haint* is the Gullah word for an evil and restless wandering spirit.)

Pat would laugh at our stories, and we'd say, "*No, no, no*, it's true!" We'd say, "Mr. Conroy, if you don't do right, we can take some of your hair and nail it to a tree and make you go crazy."

He knew we didn't know anything about

real voodoo and these were just kid stories, so one day he announced, "I've got some magic for y'all this week." He brought a lady to class whose long hair fell way below her backside. It was a science period and Pat had also brought along a magnet, a battery, and some wires . . . and he hooked it all up like the science book said. We had no idea what was going to happen, but he had our attention. He asked the lady with the hair to come to the front of the class and touch the magnet contraption. When she did, her long hair flew to the ceiling and stood straight on end—and all us eighteen kids took off toward the door screaming and running over one another to get away. We thought that lady was possessed!

He yelled for us to come back and he was laughing hard, just tickled pink with himself. He told us, "Y'all have your voodoo, but I've got my magic too."

After he taught us what his experiment that day was really about, we finally figured out that his magic was better than ours. You see, he was preparing us for things we would see and would not understand when we left the island, and not to be afraid of things we didn't understand.

Comeya Choice Bake Turkey Legs

Most people don't think about cooking the turkey legs separate from the rest of the bird, but there's a lot of dark meat on those big legs. The peppers and onions add a juicy, rich flavor to this dish.

Serves 4 to 6

4 to 6 turkey legs, cleaned and patted dry

1 tablespoon salt

1 teaspoon pepper

1 teaspoon poultry seasoning

1 tablespoon garlic powder

1 teaspoon dried thyme

1 teaspoon dried rosemary (optional)

¼ green bell pepper, diced

¼ red bell pepper, diced

2 ribs celery, diced

1 large sweet onion, diced

Preheat the oven to 365°F.

Arrange the turkey legs in a roasting pan in one layer, so that the large end of one piece faces the small end of another.

Combine the salt, pepper, poultry seasoning, garlic powder, thyme, and rosemary (if using) in a small bowl. Sprinkle this dry seasoning evenly over the turkey legs. Spread the bell peppers, celery, and onion over and around the legs. Pour 5 to 6 cups water around the turkey legs, being careful not to rinse off the seasoning.

Cover with a lid or aluminum foil and bake for 2 hours, then uncover and baste the turkey legs several times. Check for tenderness. If the meat is not tender, cover and bake for 1 hour longer. Uncover and bake for 5 to 10 minutes, until browned on top. Serve.

Grillin Turkey Breast

A turkey has two large breasts, so if you've bought the whole turkey, grill both.

Serves 4 to 6

1 or 2 boneless turkey breasts, cleaned and
   patted dry

1 tablespoon salt

1 tablespoon pepper

1 tablespoon garlic powder

1 tablespoon paprika

Prepare a charcoal grill.

Place the breasts in a shallow pan.

Combine the salt, pepper, garlic powder, and paprika in a small bowl and sprinkle or pat all over the turkey breasts.

When the grill is hot, place the seasoned turkey breast directly on the grill, and cook for 6 minutes on each side, turning with tongs, until the breast is browned all over and the meat is fork tender and the juice runs clear. A thermometer placed in the thickest part of the breast should read 160°F.

Transfer to a platter and serve with your favorite vegetables, starch, or make a great sandwich and refrigerate the leftovers.

My Pineapple Mango Turkey

If you bake the half turkey in one piece, let it rest a little after cooking before you slice. If you use turkey pieces for the recipe, there's no need to let them rest before serving.

Serves 6

1 (3- to 5-pound) half turkey, or turkey pieces, cleaned and patted dry

1 tablespoon salt

1 tablespoon pepper

3 to 4 fresh mangoes, peeled, pitted, and cut into large slices

1 (20-ounce) can pineapple chunks, with juice

2 (11.5-ounce) cans frozen pineapple juice concentrate, thawed and at room temperature

Preheat the oven to 365°F.

Place the turkey in a roasting pan. Season with salt and pepper all over, then arrange the mango and pineapple chunks around the turkey and place some in the cavity. Pour the pineapple juice around the turkey, not over it, to avoid washing off the seasoning.

Cover with a lid or aluminum foil and roast for 1½ hours, then remove the cover and baste the turkey. Cover again and bake for another 1½ hours, or until the internal temperature reaches 160°F. Uncover and roast for another 5 to 10 minutes, until browned on top. Serve.

Easy Island Turkey Meatloaf

Ground turkey is a new thing in the groceries and makes a lighter meatloaf than the traditional beef and pork, with not so much fat. If you slice the loaf while it's still hot, it will be crumbly. If you want your slices to be firmer, let it cool at room temperature for 45 minutes to 1 hour before slicing (though it tastes good even if you can't wait for it to cool).

Serves 6 to 8

1 pound ground white meat turkey

1 pound ground dark meat turkey

2 teaspoons salt

2 teaspoons pepper

2 teaspoons garlic powder

2 large eggs, beaten well

1 sweet onion, finely diced

½ medium green or red bell pepper, finely diced (optional)

1½ cups breadcrumbs

½ cup ketchup

Preheat the oven to 350°F.

Put the ground turkey in a large mixing bowl along with the salt, pepper, garlic powder, eggs, onion, bell pepper, breadcrumbs, and ¼ cup of the ketchup. Use clean hands to mix the ingredients together well.

Place the mixture in a standard loaf pan and pat the meat down well, so the top is about ¼ inch from the top of the pan. Use a spoon or squirt bottle to spread the remaining ketchup on top.

Bake for 45 minutes to 1 hour, until the center is firm. You can also test for doneness by inserting a toothpick into the middle; if it comes out clean, you are done. Let stand, then slice and serve.

Stuffin Yo Turkey Breast

This is a fancy dish that's easy to make. You don't need to save this recipe for a holiday; it's good anytime.

Serves 6

1 (3- to 5-pound) boneless turkey breast

1 teaspoon salt

1 teaspoon pepper

1 teaspoon garlic powder

Stuffing:

½ pound bacon, cooked crispy and crumbled

1 sweet onion, finely diced

1 stalk celery, finely diced

2 to 4 cups stuffing mix of your choice, such as cornbread or herb

1 teaspoon dried or chopped fresh sage

⅔ to 1 cup chicken or turkey broth

Preheat the oven to 350°F.

In a medium mixing bowl, combine all the stuffing ingredients.

Place the turkey in large roasting pan and sprinkle the salt, pepper, and garlic powder all over it.

Use a sharp knife to cut a pocket in the center of the turkey breast and add the stuffing to the pocket. Use kitchen string to tie around the breast and secure the stuffing.

Bake, uncovered, for 2½ to 3 hours. Don't baste it during the baking.

The turkey is done when a thermometer inserted in the thickest part of the breast reads 160°F.

Let the turkey cool slightly before you remove the string, slice, and serve.

I am sure there were days when Pop wished he could afford some fancy machines like a plow or a truck to haul wood that would help make the work just a little easier. Pop didn't usually mind hard work, however, and not having these conveniences never got in his way. Even though we did not have such machinery, we raised strong bulls to do much of the work, pulling the wagon for our transportation and hauling other heavy loads that we could not manage.

Most people had cows on their land. We had two cows and a horse. We had one milk cow named Sarah and one ox, Bobby, who was the work cow. We raised Bobby from two months old. Momma said she fell in love with Bobby shortly after he was born and bought him from a couple living on the island. He had a white star in the middle of his forehead. We tamed him by teaching

him how to do certain things. When we called him, he would moo to us. He knew how to back up and go forward when we told him to do so. He was smart and a great pet. We taught him to be ridden bareback like a horse when he was two years old. About once a week Pop would hitch Bobby to the wagon and take us along into the woods with him to cut down several medium-size trees. He would have us girls saw the trees into logs with hand saws. Bobby would haul the load back for firewood for our stove or our heater, which was a lot easier than pulling them ourselves.

Sarah, our milk cow, she had the biggest round eyes, with a black ring around one. Sarah was so gentle. We enjoyed getting milk from Sarah, even though that meant getting up extra early every morning to milk Sarah before her calf got started milking.

Ol' Fashion Stew Beef with Lima Beans, Peas, and Carrots

Whether you use white or red potatoes, your stew will be awesome. Timing the addition of the potatoes is most important to the success of this stew.

Serves 4 to 6

¼ cup vegetable oil

1½ pounds chuck stew beef, with a little fat, cut into bite-size cubes

1 large sweet onion, coarsely chopped

1½ ribs celery, chopped

1 (15-ounce) can tomato sauce

8 large fresh tomatoes, or 2 (14.5-ounce) cans diced tomatoes, with juice

2 to 3 teaspoons minced fresh garlic or garlic powder

2 teaspoons salt, or more to taste

2 teaspoons pepper, or more to taste

2 cups fresh or frozen green lima beans

1 cup sweet corn kernels, fresh or frozen

3 to 4 carrots, peeled and cut into thirds

4 to 6 medium white potatoes, cut in half

In a large stockpot, heat the oil over medium-high heat. When the oil is hot but not smoking, add the beef pieces slowly, stirring constantly, and fry until they are browned all over, 3 to 5 minutes total; do not cook the meat through. Pour off the excess oil from the pot and add the onion to the pot. Cook for 3 to 5 minutes, until the onion starts to turn translucent.

Stir in the celery, tomato sauce, diced tomatos, garlic, and enough water to fill the pot two-thirds full (about 4 cups). Increase the heat to medium-high, bring to a boil, cover, lower the heat to medium, and cook for 1 hour, stirring occasionally.

Add the salt, pepper, lima beans, and corn and continue to cook for 45 minutes.

Add the carrots and potatoes, and check to see if the beef is tender. Cook for 30 minutes more, then taste to check the seasoning. Add more if needed. Reduce the heat to low to keep warm until you are ready to serve, and stir on occasion to keep the stew from sticking.

Momma and Pop

As time moved along, Momma would pay closer attention to my sisters and me becoming young ladies, suspecting, I guess, that we would soon be leaving home and our way of life would change. But before we went, she wanted to make sure that we was as ready as we could get. Momma would take off her apron, sit in her favorite chair in a corner, and call us over to gather around her and listen to what she had to say. Momma would look at each one of us and then call out our name. Then she would say, "I want yah ta undahstand dat when yah leave yah and go ovah yondah for school, yah need ta be on yo best behavior, cause I say so. Don't tink when yah leave I want know what yah doing cause I will. I know plenty people ovah dah jus like here who will let me know and I will be da wit me stick. And iffa I have to come, it be you and me. Y'all not gonna leave yah and make me shame, so yah betta do dah right ting. I send yah ta get yo ed-u-macation, not ta play." Our folks never gave up on teaching and encouraging us so that we would know the meaning of "you don't miss your water until your well runs dry." Something we just didn't have a clue about at such a young age. But they did know that when the time come for us to use their lessons, we would be reminded of their words.

I later realized that being a parent was much harder than I could ever imagine. Native folks knew what they had to do—what was important, when it was time for important decisions, and that time was of the essence. Folks never stopped trying to instill in us that a "change was gonna come, and us chillen had bettah get ready." They had a kind of belief that was not easily shaken and a kind of pride that stood the test of time. They worked hard to make their dreams become goals and goals become reality, hoping we would be strong and follow in their footsteps. What little they had they were proud of, and nuttin else really mattered.

Sometimes, Pop would put us through tests to see if we were paying attention to what they were trying to teach us. He would surprise us with one of his questions he had asked before, but would make it sound different. He would sit there and look at us while we kids were trying to figure out the answer. Momma would hear the question and wait to see how long it took for us to answer. And even if we didn't know the answer we knew we had to say something. Then she would come from the kitchen and say: "Bein grown ain't all what y'all tink it tis. Y'all chillens gottah long way ta go and a short time to make it." Then she would say: "Look at yah! Yah milk ain't dried up from round yah mout yet."

We knew it was best for us to be quiet while one of them was talking—and we sure couldn't laugh. My sisters and I would stay frozen and let Momma finish before saying "Wee don' tink dat wee be grown" and leave it at that. We knew that the less words said the better off we would be. Many times it seemed to us that they were throwing words at us that had no meaning. There were times when it seemed as if Momma and Pop just wanted to hear themselves talk. But no matter what we were feeling or thinking at that time, one thing was for sure: Our crazy feelings were best kept to ourselves, our mouths shut and our ears open.

Now I realize more than ever why our folks pushed us so hard to know the things that they were teaching us. Making sure that we got a good education was very important to Pop and Momma because they had so little and at times wished they had more.

One benefit we had that is a problem for kids today: We knew nothing about peer pressure, or sayin we were bored and ain't nuttin to do. Every kid on the island worked with their parents and families for survival. Envy and jealousy over possessions or social standing or money were virtually nonexistent.

In our simple ways, Daufuskie was our own Garden of Eden. Our needs were met, and we shared all that it took to be a family who worked together and enjoyed rewards. I try hard never to forget to give thanks for all things that come, go, or linger along my way, big or small. And I try to keep my mind and attitude positive about all things.

Our folks made sure that they got our attention because they knew that we needed to learn all that they had to pass on. We once lived our island lives without the need of progress, but, as it entered, we learned that time was changing. Our parents enriched our minds and bodies with stories of long-ago ancestors, wisdom, and knowledge—and really great food!

Yondah Beef Stew with Corn and Sweet Peas

This stew is good in August when you can get fresh corn and peas. Of course, it's great in the winter, too, just substitute frozen corn and peas.

Serves 6

2 to 3 tablespoon oil

1½ pounds stew beef, cubed

1 large sweet onion, diced

1 rib celery, diced

½ red bell pepper, diced

½ green bell pepper, diced

1 teaspoon salt

1 teaspoon pepper

2 to 3 ears corn, shucked and cut into 1-inch pieces

1½ quarts beef stock or water

1 cup fresh shelled sweet peas

Steamed rice, for serving (optional)

In a large stewpot, heat the oil over medium heat, then add the beef and sear until the pieces just begin to brown, 3 to 5 minutes. Add the onion, celery, and bell peppers and cook for 2 to 3 minutes, stirring constantly. Season with salt and pepper, add the corn and stock, and cover. Cook over medium-high heat for 1½ hours, or until the beef is tender.

Add the peas and cook for another 20 to 30 minutes.

Serve in bowls, or over rice.

Beenyah Soul Pot Roast with Potatoes, Carrots, and Peas

The bigger pieces of potato in this recipe ensure that the potato doesn't break down and become mushy during cooking. I like to cut up the potato in my plate as I'm eating the pot roast.

Serves 6 to 8

¼ cup canola or vegetable oil

1 (5- to 6-pound) beef chuck roast

½ cup all-purpose flour

2 tablespoons salt

2 tablespoons pepper

2 tablespoons minced garlic

1 large onion, diced

½ green bell pepper, diced

½ red bell pepper, diced

1 teaspoon fresh or dried thyme

3 large white potatoes, each cut into 3 pieces

3 large carrots, each cut into 4 pieces

1 cup fresh or frozen shelled sweet peas

In a large stock or stewpot, heat the oil over medium-high heat, then add the roast. Cook for 6 to 8 minutes on each side, until slightly browned. Remove the roast and set aside, leaving the oil in the pot. Add the flour to the pot and stir over medium heat until the flour browns. Return the roast to the pot and add the salt, pepper, garlic, onion, bell peppers, thyme, and enough water to cover the vegetables, about 1 cup. Bring to a boil, then reduce the heat to medium-low and cover. Cook for 1½ to 2½ hours, until the meat is tender. At that point, add the potatoes, carrots, and peas and continue to cook, stirring occasionally, for 20 to 30 minutes, until the vegetables are tender but not mushy.

Recipe for dah Soul

One handful of RESPECT

Do to others as you would want them to do to you

Two scoops of BELIEF

Never set limits; reach for the brightest star

Three pinches of VALUE

Don't just live life, treasure the life you live

Four dashes of tough LOVE

Listen and learn, then survive the challenges that comes your way

Unlimited amount of SMILES and LAUGHTER

Priceless, painless, and free

Combine these ingredients with self-control and take each day as it comes. Be thankful and proud for all that you do and accomplish. And remember that when tomorrow comes, you will see that yesterday was your blessing for being a part of today.

Blossom Beef Rump Roast with Gravy

Everyone called my beloved grandmomma Louvenia by her nickname, "Blossom." This was one of the many great recipes that she enjoyed cooking. She loved cooking with the vegetables from her garden, and she always gave extra vegetables to her neighbors.

Serves 6 to 8

2 to 3 tablespoons vegetable oil

2 teaspoons self-rising flour

1 (3- to 5-pound) beef chuck roast

1 large sweet onion, diced

½ green bell pepper, diced

½ red bell pepper, diced

1 heaping teaspoon dried thyme

3 cloves garlic, minced

2 to 3 cups hot water

Salt and pepper to taste

In a large stockpot, heat the oil over medium heat. When the oil is hot, stir in the flour and cook until it browns—this will be your roux. Reduce the heat to medium and place the roast in the pot and flip it a few times to coat with the roux. Cook for 2 minutes on each side, then add the onion, bell peppers, thyme, and garlic and stir together. Add the hot water, stir, cover, and cook for 2 hours. Check every 30 minutes for tenderness. It may take longer to get a fork-tender roast. Be patient. The longer you slow cook a roast, the better it will taste. As the gravy thickens, you may need to add more hot water. A good gravy slides off a spoon rather than drips from it.

Serve the roast in a serving dish with the gravy around it.

Country Fried Steak with Brown Gravy

I recommend using cube steaks because they are already beaten at the butcher to loosen up the muscles, which ensures your steaks will be tender.

Serves 4 to 6

1½ cups vegetable oil

4 to 6 cube steaks

1 tablespoon salt, plus more to taste

1 tablespoon pepper, plus more to taste

1 tablespoon garlic powder

1½ cups plus 2 tablespoons self-rising flour

½ cup hot water

In a large skillet, heat the oil over medium-high heat until hot but not smoking.

Lay the cube steaks on a sheet pan or on a clean flat surface and season by sprinkling each side evenly with a combination of the salt, pepper, and garlic powder.

Sprinkle the 1½ cups flour over the steaks, or dredge them in flour to coat well on both sides. Shake off excess flour and fry one steak at a time in the hot oil for 2 to 4 minutes on each side, until it is slightly browned on both sides. Remove each steak to a flat pan as you cook, repeating the process until all the steaks are cooked.

Pour off all but 2 tablespoons of the oil from the skillet and place the skillet back on the stove over medium heat. Add the 2 tablespoons flour to the oil in the skillet, stirring constantly with fork or wooden spoon as the flour browns. When the flour turns medium brown, add the hot water and continue to stir as gravy forms and slightly thickens. Lower the heat, season the gravy with salt and pepper, and cook for about 30 minutes. Place the steaks on a platter, pour brown gravy on top to cover, and enjoy.

Braised Beef Short Ribs and Baby Carrots

Do not wash the beef short ribs. Washing makes fresh beef tough. You need to wash pork or chicken, but not steak.

Serves 4 to 6

¼ cup vegetable oil

3 to 4 pounds beef short ribs, cut apart

2 to 3 teaspoons salt

2 to 3 teaspoons pepper

1 tablespoon garlic powder

1 onion, diced

12 to 16 whole baby carrots

In a large heavy-bottom pot or Dutch oven, heat the oil over medium-high heat. Use tongs to place the short ribs in the hot oil and fry for 1 to 2 minutes on each side. Remove to a pan.

Pour off the oil from the pot, return the short ribs to the pot, and stir in the salt, pepper, garlic powder, and onion. Add ½ cup water, then cover and cook over medium heat for 45 minutes. The ribs will not be tender yet.

Meanwhile, preheat the oven to 365°F.

Place the ribs in a roasting pan or large casserole, cover with a lid or aluminum foil, and bake for 1 hour. Add the carrots and bake for 15 to 20 minutes more, until tender.

Southern Comfort Oxtail

When you buy oxtail from a supermarket, it is usually cut up into thick slices, whereas if you go to a butcher you can get your oxtail whole and have them cut it up as thick or thin as you want. I usually get mine from the butcher, cut into ¼-inch-thick pieces; because oxtail takes hours to cook, a thinner slice like this won't take quite as long to become tender. You may choose to cook oxtail in a slow cooker, a heavy pot on the stovetop, or in a roasting pan in the oven. It's up to you. This version is for the stovetop.

Serves 4 to 6

½ cup vegetable oil

3 to 4 pounds oxtail (do not wash because it toughens the meat)

2 large sweet onions, diced

½ large red bell pepper, diced

½ large green bell pepper, diced

1 tablespoon salt, or more to taste

2 teaspoons pepper, or more to taste

Hot water

In a large soup pot, heat the oil over medium-high heat. When the oil is hot but not smoking, add the oxtail and fry for 2 to 3 minutes on each side, until the oxtail is beginning to brown.

Pour off the grease from the pot, and put the onion and bell peppers into the pot. Stir in the salt and pepper, then add enough hot water to fill the pot one-third full. Stir again, cover, and cook over medium-high heat, stirring on occasion and scraping up any browned bits in the pot, for at least 3½ hours, until tender. After 1½ hours, check and add hot water if needed. The liquid should cover the oxtail while cooking, to keep it from sticking to the pot.

If it isn't tender at this point, lower the heat to medium and continue to cook, covered, until the oxtail is tender.

Check the seasoning while cooking and add more salt and pepper if needed.

My Golly Oxtail with Green Lima Beans

The green lima beans add a thickness to the sauce in the pot and are a great flavor to pair with oxtail.

Serves 4 to 6

¼ cup vegetable oil

3 pounds oxtail (do not wash because it toughens the meat)

1 large sweet onion, diced

1 tablespoon salt

1 tablespoon pepper

Hot water

1 pound fresh green lima beans

In a stockpot, heat the oil over medium-high heat, then add the oxtail and fry for 15 to 20 minutes, turning to sear the pieces all over. Stir in the onion, salt, and pepper. Add enough hot water to cover the meat and cook for at least 2½ hours, stirring on occasion. When the meat is fork tender, reduce the heat to medium, add the lima beans to the pot, along with more hot water as needed to cover the meat and beans. Cook for another 30 to 45 minutes, stirring on occasion, or until the oxtail and beans are both tender and tasty. Do not add more water.

We Are Family (Dem Dawn Bloodline)

Momma loved her family and believed that we needed to know who our people were on both her and Pop's sides, going as far back as she could remember. She would make sure that we knew the ones who were dead, the living who were in cities far away, and especially those just cross the way in Savannah. And believe me, she could talk for hours about them all. As I sat and listened and learned, I sometime got caught up and would ask more questions. I often wondered how she remembered all those folks in her head even after having a stroke years earlier.

I remember one day while Momma was talking about family I asked her, "At what point do the blood runs out from a relative who is way-down kin folks, like fifth, sixth, and seventh cousin?" Momma paused and gave me a hard look and said, "Wa yah fo mean, chile? Family be family always, and nevah evah stop being family no mattar how far down they may be . . . In otta fo us ta be here now, somebody from way yondah started us. Dah ain't no such ting as not kin ta yah. Fo if da wasn't fo da ones in da beginning, den da wouldn't be none of us ta go on. Way yah foget dat from? Wasn't yah ears open when I be talkin ta yah?"

I didn't have any quick answer when she asked, so I just said, "Yes ma'am, I was jus askin." Momma looked at me even closer and made it clear: "Dare is no ending to da beginning of something we don't know bout, cept family be forever. Bloodline is bout people dat been born and bound together cause of da one long before of long ago. Whether someone is yo first or de twentyish, dey be family . . . fo dats what bloodline be bout. Being related is someting you can't change once yah born, no mattar how yah feel bout any of dem." Then she reminded me, "You can pick yo friends, but yah can't choose yo family."

I do believe that was the Gullah folks' way of keeping us from dating when we were kids, by saying we all be family. And their reasons were probably pretty good; the raising of eight girls was a handful enough.

Beenyah Oxtail, Tomato, and Okra

This recipe is like a stew. I like to pre-fry the okra so it isn't slimy and holds its texture better.

Serves 4 to 6

4 tablespoons vegetable oil

2 pounds oxtail, in ¼-inch-thick pieces

1 large onion, chopped

2 (14.5-ounce) cans diced tomatoes with juice; or 6 to 8 fresh tomatoes, diced

2 teaspoons salt

2 teaspoons pepper

1 pound fresh okra, rinsed, or frozen okra, sliced ¼ inch thick (or thicker if you like)

In a stockpot, heat 2 tablespoons of the oil over medium-high heat. When the oil is hot but not smoking, carefully place the oxtail in the oil and fry for 2 to 3 minutes on each side, or until it browns.

Add the onion and cook, stirring, for 2 to 3 minutes. Stir in the tomatoes, salt, pepper, and enough hot water to half fill the pot.

Lower the heat to medium and cook for 2½ hours, stirring on occasion to keep the meat from sticking. As the oxtail cooks, you may need to add 1 cup or more hot water and a pinch more salt if needed to keep the water above the meat.

When the oxtail is fork tender, reduce the heat to low while you fry your okra.

In a skillet, heat the remaining 2 tablespoons oil over medium heat and add the okra. Fry lightly, for 3 to 5 minutes. Transfer to paper towels to drain, then add the okra to the oxtail.

Increase the heat to medium and cook for about 15 minutes, until the okra is tender and tasty.

Southern Smuttered Liver and Onion

Momma and Pop loved eating all kinds of liver—hog, chicken, deer, rabbit, and squirrel—and most times with grits.

Serves 4 to 6

1 cup vegetable oil

4 to 6 slices beef or pork liver

1 teaspoon salt

1 teaspoon pepper

1 teaspoon garlic powder

1 teaspoon paprika

1 cup self-rising flour

1 large onion, sliced into ¼-inch-thick rings

In a large skillet, heat the oil over medium heat until hot but not smoking.

In a small bowl, combine the salt, pepper, garlic powder, and paprika and season each piece of liver on both sides.

Put the flour in a separate bowl, and dredge each piece of liver in the flour, one at a time, then shake off excess flour.

Fry the liver in batches; do not crowd the skillet. Cook for 2 minutes on each side, or until browned. Transfer to a plate and keep warm.

Add the onion rings to the oil in the pan and cook for 3 to 5 minutes, until the onion is translucent. Use a slotted spoon to remove the onion to a plate or bowl, pour off the oil from the skillet, and place the liver back in the skillet. Spoon the onion atop the liver. Add ⅔ cup water, lower the heat to medium-low, and simmer for 10 to 15 minutes, until the gravy thickens. Keep warm over low heat until ready to serve.

Hog-Killin Time

Lots of things we did growing up were fun mixed with hard work. Hog-killin time was one of those events. It was also an experience we had to be a part of, even us girls. Today when I look back I can see and hear the voices of native folks coming together for pre-planning days before the big throwdown. Momma couldn't wait to get those chitlins, liver, heart, and a piece of fresh bacon so she could rush off to the kitchen and prepare suppers for us with some grits or sweet potato. We used every part of the hog, from the head to the foot.

Here is how killin time happens: The talk is all ovah the island for weeks bout Thomas and Bertha fixin ta kill dat big hundred-pound hog da got. My sisters and I are busy making sure lots and lots of water be pumped, and enough firewood collected. Momma would also have us dig a hole in the backyard for when she was ready to clean the chitlins.

The day come, and the knives are sharpened, and about three or four of Pop's men friends show up at daybreak. The collected firewood is set under a number 3 wash tub with enough water to be boil. The men start talking about how long it should take to kill, clean, and hang the hog in the backyard from the mulberry tree. Much work had to be done for the entire process—the hog has to be hanged in the tree and allowed to drain for about two or three hours alone, and everything has to be done before sundown.

Once the hog has been hanged and secured up high in the mulberry tree, the men then takes their conversations to the back porch. Meanwhile, Momma is in the kitchen getting ready to prepare the fresh liver given to her shortly after the cleaning. By the time the hog has drained and is ready to be cut up, Momma sends out her big dish pan to collect much of the fat that would be kept for frying other meat later. Pop and his friends unhang the hog, and they lay it on its back on a clean flat surface. Using a hatchet and sharp knife to cut through the bones and thick meat, they first cut the hog into four quarters, then cut each portion into smaller pieces. Some of the larger parts of the hog are placed in a big wooden box, layered in salt, sealed, and put in our corner house (a little wooden house in the backyard used for storage) for weeks until the meat is cured.

After all the cutting, Pop makes sure his friends who helped get to take home a nice piece, and he also had pieces to give out to folks who couldn't raise hog for themselves, and a few family members. For us, we would have enough fresh salted pork meat to last through the winter months and sometime up to the beginning of summer. For the first week or two after killing the hog, Momma would cook pork as many ways as she could, until Pop would go and catch some fresh mullets for a change in meal.

Momma's Smuttered Pork Spare Ribs

We loved eating ribs with gravy as children. They're tender and tasty and go really well with mashed potatoes. Forget the barbecue sauce!

Serves 4 to 6

1 slab pork babyback ribs, cut into single ribs

2 teaspoons salt, or to taste

2 teaspoons pepper, or to taste

2 to 3 teaspoons garlic powder

2 teaspoons paprika

1 tablespoon poultry seasoning (optional)

2 cups self-rising flour

3 cups vegetable oil

¼ green bell pepper, diced

¼ red bell pepper, diced

½ rib celery, diced

Rinse the ribs, pat them dry, and put them in a large bowl. Season with 1 teaspoon salt, 1 teaspoon pepper, the garlic powder, paprika, and poultry seasoning (if using) and toss to coat well.

Put the flour in a gallon-size plastic or paper bag, add 4 to 6 ribs at a time, and shake to coat well. Shake to remove excess flour before frying.

In a large skillet, heat the oil over medium-high heat. Check the oil to make sure it is hot by putting a pinch of flour in hot oil. If it floats, the oil is not ready for frying, but if the flour sizzles, you are ready to fry. Fry the ribs in batches, so you don't crowd the skillet, for 3 to 4 minutes on each side, or until browned. Transfer from the skillet to drain on a platter lined with paper towels. Repeat the process until all the ribs are fried. Season with 1 teaspoon salt and 1 teaspoon black pepper, or to taste.

Pour off any remaining oil from the skillet, return the fried ribs to the skillet, and spread the bell peppers and celery on top. Add enough water to barely cover the ribs and vegetables. Season with salt and pepper, and partially cover the skillet, leaving a small opening so the contents won't boil over. Turn the heat to medium-high and cook for 20 minutes, or until the gravy slightly thickens (add extra water if needed), then decrease the heat to low. Cook for 20 to 30 minutes, basting the ribs occasionally with the gravy, until the meat and vegetables are fork tender. Taste and adjust the seasoning as desired. Serve.

Bake Pork Chops with Apple Bread Stuffin

If you have leftover cornbread, break it up and use that in place of the cornbread croutons.

Serves 4 to 6

Apple Bread Stuffin (recipe follows)

4 to 6 (1-inch-thick) pork chops

1 tablespoon salt

1 tablespoon pepper

1 tablespoon garlic powder

1 teaspoon fresh or dried thyme

Divide the stuffing into 4 to 6 equal portions.

Wash and pat dry the pork chops, then make a 2-inch incision, cutting into the side of the meaty area, to create a pocket for the stuffing.

Fill each pocket with a portion of stuffing, and season the pork chops on both sides with salt, pepper, garlic powder, and thyme. Refrigerate until ready to cook. (These can be stuffed in the morning and cooked in the evening. If you do so, remove from the refrigerator 30 minutes before cooking to return the chops to room temperature.)

When you are ready to cook, preheat the oven to 400°F.

Arrange the chops in a large baking pan in one layer and bake for 30 minutes, or until the chops begin to brown and are fork tender.

Apple Bread Stuffin

4 green apples

4 tablespoons (½ stick) butter

1 rib celery, diced

1 large onion, diced

½ teaspoon minced garlic

2 cups cornbread croutons, or leftover cornbread

⅔ cup chicken broth

Wash and core but do not peel the apples, then finely dice them.

In a skillet, heat the butter over medium-high heat and stir to melt. Add the celery, onion, garlic, and apples and cook for 3 to 4 minutes, stirring. Remove from the heat and transfer the mixture into a large bowl along with the croutons and broth. Stir well to combine, and let the croutons soak up the liquid.

Fresh Bake Pork Roast with Sweet Potatoes

Instead of pairing this pork roast with apples, I like to give sweetness to the dish with the addition of sweet potatoes.

Serves 6 to 8

1 (4- to 5-pound) pork roast (shoulder or ham)

1 tablespoon salt

1 tablespoon pepper

2 tablespoons minced garlic

1 tablespoon dried thyme

3 to 4 sweet potatoes, peeled and cut in half

Preheat the oven to 350°F.

Rinse and pat the roast dry. Place it in a roasting pan.

Combine the salt, pepper, garlic, and thyme in a bowl and sprinkle or pat over the entire roast.

Add 2 cups water to the roasting pan, cover tightly with a lid or aluminum foil, and roast for 2 hours, basting several times, until the meat is tender.

Arrange the sweet potatoes around the roast and continue to roast for 30 to 45 minutes, or until the potatoes are tender.

Uncover and cook for 10 minutes, or until the roast is slightly browned on top. Serve.

Hooked, Trapped, and Netted

Seafood is a big part of a Gullah diet, and I grew up eating the freshest shrimp, crab, fish, conchs, clams, and—most of all—oysters. All these were cooked with a touch of love for the hard work given. I never knew how blessed we were in having the purest food of sea and land. As children, we simply didn't know that others beyond us didn't always have it our way!

Folks always had great times on Daufuskie, but meeting at the county dock at Benjie's Point with our handmade twine fishing lines, crab drop nets, and dip nets was tops. Folks would come out just as the tide was halfway down. Everyone had their certain lucky spot, whether on the dock or spread out on the oyster banks nearby. Fishing was a great time to gather with family and neighbors to catch that night's supper or tomorrow morning's breakfast, served fried over some hot grits. One after another, someone would yell out, "I got one." Hopefully it be some fish we eat, like whiting, trout, croaker, shark, eel, flounder, drum, or bass. We didn't care to eat a dogfish or a stingray. Sometime the biting gnats would be swarm all over us even as we tried swatting them away. Older folks believed that when the gnats were bad while fishing, it was a sign that the fishing would be

good. Sometimes we'd compete to see who would catch the biggest fish and have bragging rights until our next meet-up.

Crabbing is a waiting game like fishing, but a different way of catching your dinner. We used a wire drop trap baited with a piece of meat, such as chicken neck, chicken back, or any unwanted piece of fish tied on a string. It takes courage to remove blue crab from the crab trap. Once caught, crabs become very defensive, using their two big claws to reach up at you as you pull them up out of the water in the trap, open the trap door, and try to remove them. Best way I know to remove a crab from the trap is to first have on some thick rubber gloves so as to hold down the crab without getting bitten directly. Grab the crab's two last back fins, holding them tightly from behind while keeping the snapping claws away from you; it will try to wiggle out of your hand, so watch out!

Sometime folks would gather at the dock to meet the big shrimp boats and purchase baskets of crabs and shrimps to resell. And when we weren't at the county dock, sometime we would meet up at the Bloody Point beach with buckets to dig for the clams and conchs there—Momma's recipe for them made the best meals!

Belly-Fillin Carolina Country Boil

If you wanted to cook a larger amount, you would normally cook it outside over an open fire, and in a bigger pot. Live crabs can't get out of a deep basket, so you can use that to hold them until they are ready to go in the pot. You can also hold them under running hot water, and it will slow their movements.

Serves 8 to 10

⅓ to ½ cup crab boil seasoning

5 ears corn, shucked and cut in half

2 pounds smoked link sausage, cut into 2-inch lengths

1 to 2 pounds small red potatoes, skin on

1 dozen live crabs

2 to 3 pounds extra-large raw shrimp, heads on

1 dozen clams (optional)

Lemon wedges, for serving

Fill a large stockpot one-third full of water and bring to a boil over high heat. Stir in the crab boil seasoning, add the corn and smoked sausage, and cook for 10 minutes. Next add the crabs (use tongs to carefully handle the crabs), stir, and cook for 5 minutes. Add the potatoes and cook for 3 to 4 minutes, then add the shrimp (and clams, if using) and cook for 3 to 4 minutes, stirring, until the shrimp are pink and the clams have opened. Turn off the heat and let the pot sit on the burner for about 2 minutes to cool slightly. Use a large strainer to transfer the sausage, seafood, and vegetables to a big bowl or serving platter. Serve with lemon wedges.

Broken Blue Crab Stew

If you have never debarked and cleaned a live crab, know that you should be very careful not to get bitten. You can stun them by dipping them in a pot of hot water before you debark. And, of course, break off the claws first.

To eat this dish, use your fingers or a fork to pick the crabmeat out of the shells. The gravy is really good with cornbread, too.

Serves 4 to 6

3 to 4 strips smoke bacon

2 tablespoons self-rising flour

6 live blue crabs, dipped in a pot of hot water to stun, then debarked (see page 97), cleaned, and broken in half

1 onion, diced

Salt and pepper to taste

Lemon wedges, for serving

In a skillet over medium heat, fry the bacon until crispy and set aside, leaving the bacon fat in the skillet. Stir the flour into the bacon fat and cook until it browns. Add the crab halves, bacon, onion, and salt and pepper to taste to the skillet, stir several times, then stir in 2 to 3 cups hot water and cover tightly. Increase the heat to medium-high and bring to a boil, then reduce the heat to medium and cook for 20 minutes, or until the gravy thickens slightly. You can simmer over low heat until you're ready to serve. Serve with lemon wedges.

'Fuskie Shrimp and Blue Crab Burger

You can eat these tasty burgers on buns or just by themselves with a little tartar sauce.

Serves 8

1½ cups vegetable oil

1 pound small raw shrimp, peeled and deveined

1 pound lump crabmeat, loosened or picked through

½ onion, finely diced

1 to 2 teaspoons salt

1 to 2 teaspoons pepper

1 to 2 teaspoons garlic powder

2 tablespoons melted butter or vegetable oil

2 tablespoons self-rising flour

For serving (optional):

Lemon wedges

8 hamburger buns

Mayonnaise or tartar sauce

Pickles, tomatoes, and cheese (optional)

Heat the oil in a large skillet over medium-high heat until hot, but not smoking.

In a large mixing bowl, combine the shrimp, crabmeat, onion, salt, pepper, garlic powder, butter, and flour and mix well.

Divide the mixture into 8 portions and use your hands to form them into patties.

Fry 4 patties at a time for 3 to 4 minutes on each side, or until golden brown on both sides. Drain the patties on a platter lined with paper towels.

Put the burgers on buns with your favorite garnishes or eat by themselves, and enjoy.

Dah Way We Gather Food from dah River

Some days after a big catch, Mom and Pop would bring home several bushels of blue crabs from the boat, so we had to get busy. First we had to gather lots of wood to start and keep the fire going, then we had to pump enough water to wash the crabs and to boil them. When the crabs were cooked, Pop would scoop them from the hot water and spread them out on several pieces of tin to cool. We got to sit around and eat a few before picking. Depending on the time of year, if it was too hot or too buggy, we would pick the crabs inside the house or outside on the porch. We kids only got to pick the claws, because Pop and Mom felt we could not pick the crab bodies close enough to get all the meat.

Blue crabs is tasty, and some would say sweet, when boiled with just a hint of salt. Here's a quick salad recipe: Use a pound of mixed crab meat (white and dark) with 2 diced hard-boiled eggs, diced ½ rib celery, 1 tablespoon sweet salad cubes, and 1 tablespoon mayonnaise (more or less). Combine and serve on a bed of lettuce or on crackers. If you like it spicy, add some type of pepper of choice or any other seasoning to give it that kick you prefer. You can also boil crabs and add different kinds of spices such as seafood boil, garlic, or any hot pepper you like. And if you want it the Gullah way, add some smoke neck bones to the water and boil for 35 to 45 minutes before adding live crabs.

Boiled Shrimps

You can catch a fish with a hook, but you will need a cast net to catch all those tasty shrimps. I love shrimp cooked several ways—fried, smothered—but if you want them in a hurry, boil them. It takes 3 to 6 minutes depending on how you like them cooked.

To cook a pound of large shrimp, fill a medium pot about one-quarter full of water and bring to a boil. Add 1 teaspoon salt, 1 teaspoon pepper, 1 tablespoon garlic powder (or minced fresh garlic) and stir. Add the shrimp and cook, stirring several times, for 3 to 5 minutes. Remove from the heat and let sit in the seasoned water for a few minutes, then drain. Then you eat 'em up one by one.

Steam Oysters

I am not a big fan of eating oysters raw—maybe because we ate so much raw growing

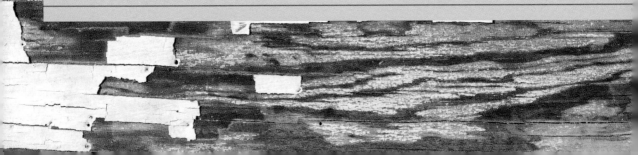

up. Other ways to cook them are fried, stewed, steamed, or baked. Oysters are seasonal starting after the first frost in October; as you may have been told, they are only good to eat in months with an *R* in the name.

To steam oysters, make a fire and close in two sides with bricks or cement blocks. Place a piece of tin across the bricks for a shelf, then add some raw oysters on top and cover with a wet burlap sack or something similar. Keep the fire hot, and the oysters will pop open when done.

Steam Clams

Clams are tasty, but they do get chewy when boiled too long. The smaller ones are more chewable than the larger ones. We used to go on the beach at low tide and dig them out of the mud, finding buckets full of various sizes. They make great chowder. We cooked clams in a large pot on the stove, with enough water to just cover the shells. We cooked them just until they opened. *Steaming* was not a word we ever used for cooking.

Crispy Fried Fish

Fried fish is good served with grits, rice, or potatoes. It's great on a sandwich as well.

Serves 4 to 6

1½ cups vegetable oil

4 to 6 pieces fish fillets of your choice (I like whiting, trout, or grouper)

1 tablespoon salt

1 tablespoon pepper

2 tablespoons paprika

1 cup self-rising flour

Lemon wedges, for serving

Heat the oil in a large skillet over medium-high heat, until the oil is hot but not smoking.

Combine the salt, pepper, and paprika in a large bowl.

Rinse the fish and pat dry. Place the fish on a pan or platter and sprinkle them generously with the dry seasoning, then flip them and sprinkle again until they are evenly seasoned. Put the flour in a large resealable bag, add 2 to 4 pieces of seasoned fish, and toss to coat.

Use a spatula to carefully place one piece of fish at a time in the hot oil and fry for 3 to 4 minutes on each side, until golden brown. For a crispy texture on the outside, turn the fish at least two times and cook for a few minutes longer.

Transfer to a platter lined with paper towels to drain. Repeat with the remaining fish pieces and serve with lemon wedges.

Grandmomma's Seafood Gumbo

Grandmomma loved her okra. She was good at making dem grow and she had a way of cooking dem up. Okra Gumbo is a favorite comfort food dat folks loves in dah South. Put yo apron on, get out yo big pot, and start cooking!

Serves 8 to 10

10 to 12 whole ripe tomatoes, diced; or 2 (14.5-ounce) cans diced tomatoes

½ (6-ounce) can tomato paste

1 cup fresh green lima beans

1 cup whole fresh corn kernels cut from the cob

1 large onion, diced

1 celery rib, diced

2 cloves garlic, minced

1 teaspoon dried thyme

½ pound lump crabmeat, loosened or picked through

½ pound claw crabmeat

½ pound raw small clams (removed from the shells)

1 pint raw oysters, shucked and drained

Salt and pepper to taste

1½ pounds medium-large raw shrimp, heads removed, peeled and deveined

1 pound fresh okra, stemmed and cut into 3 or 4 pieces each

In a large pot, combine the tomatoes, tomato paste, lima beans, corn, onion, celery, garlic, and thyme. Add 4 to 5 cups water and bring to a boil over medium-high heat. Cook, covered, for 30 to 45 minutes, then add the lump crabmeat and claw crabmeat, clams, oysters, and salt and pepper. Cook for 20 to 30 minutes more, then decrease the heat to medium and add the shrimp and okra. Check and correct the seasoning, cover, and cook for another 20 minutes. Stir in a little more water if the gumbo gets too thick.

Picking and Shucking Oysters Was Big Business

Picking and shucking oysters was big business on Daufuskie from the 1880s and into the 1950s. It was hard work with very little pay, but folks never minded—or at least never complained—because that was the way things were for them.

My great-grandmother Sally Bentley was an oyster shucker, and her husband, Charlie Bentley, was a picker (gatherer). All kinds of folks spoke highly of my great-grandmomma, remembering that she was always a hard worker, whether it was tending her fields, chopping wood for cooking or the fireplace, working in her garden, or shucking oysters at the factory that used to be on the island. Charlie Bentley, my great-grandfather, was born in 1875 and worked on a dredge in the Savannah River as well as spending time as an oyster picker and a farmer.

The creeks, bays, and sounds around the lowcountry were teeming with oysters, and Daufuskie and nearby Bluffton were the center of the oyster business; today Bluffton Oyster Company still provides oyster to the folks in the lowcountry and nearby neighbors. Both Sally and Charlie, like many other native islanders, were members of the Oyster Union Society Hall on Daufuskie back in dah day. Charlie and the other local men would go out in their small bateau boats at low tide and gather loads of oysters and then return and unload them at the operating company on Daufuskie. Sally and the other women folks would sometime spend all day from sunrise to sunset shucking oysters by the gallon.

Growing up on Daufuskie, many stories were told about the two oyster factories that once provided many gallons of oysters to Savannah to be shipped elsewhere in the United States. I'm told that each day when the women folks finished shucking, the oysters would be shipped by boat across the sound to the city market in Savannah, Georgia. Momma remembered when the price for a gallon of large oysters was about 50 to 60 cents, and the smaller oysters went for 30 to 40 cents a gallon. Wow! One single oyster costs more than that today. The oyster factories and canning on Daufuskie (Maggioni and Cetchovich) was long gone by the time I was born, yet years later we kids on the island played in the remains of the last oyster factory. It amazed me to play in a building where my great-grandparents worked long, hard hours with little pay. But through all the tuff times folks made do with what they had, and did it well.

Grand Seafood Platter

Some family likes fried fish, some likes broiled. You can choose which method you prefer to use, but this recipe is for fried seafood.

Serves 6 to 8

3 to 4 cups canola oil, or vegetable oil

4 (4- to 6-ounce) flounder or trout fillets, cleaned

1 pound raw shrimp, peeled and deveined, with tails left on

1 pound raw scallops, drained

1 pound raw shucked oysters, drained

4 teaspoons salt

2 teaspoons pepper

3 teaspoons garlic powder

1 teaspoon chili powder

2 to 3 cups self-rising flour

Lemon wedges, for serving

Heat the oil in a large skillet or deep fryer until the oil is hot but not smoking.

Combine the fish, shrimp, scallops, and oysters in a large bowl with the salt, pepper, garlic powder, and chili powder and toss to coat with the seasonings.

Put the flour in a resealable bag (or a brown bag). Add the seasoned seafood 1 or 2 handfuls at a time to the bag and shake well to coat with flour. Use a large mesh strainer to scoop out the seafood and shake off the excess flour. Use tongs to slip the seafood carefully into the hot oil and fry on each side for 1 to 2 minutes, until slightly brown. Remove and drain on a platter lined with paper towels. Repeat the process until all the seafood is cooked.

Serve on a large platter with lemon wedges and let everyone help themselves.

Crab, Okra, and Tomato Stew

Serves 4 to 6

4 thick slices bacon

1 large onion, diced

8 tomatoes, crushed; or 2 (14.5-ounce) cans diced tomatoes

½ teaspoon sugar

1 teaspoon salt, or more to taste

1 teaspoon pepper, or more to taste

½ pound dark (claw) crabmeat

½ pound white lump crabmeat

1 pound fresh okra, cut into 2 or 3 pieces each

In a large pot over medium heat, fry the bacon until crisp. Remove from the pot and set aside, leaving the bacon grease in the pot. Add the onion to the pot and cook for 3 to 5 minutes, until translucent. Add the tomatoes, sugar, salt, pepper, and 2 to 3 cups water, stir, and cook for 30 minutes.

Add the claw and lump crabmeat and cook for 20 minutes, stirring on occasion, then add the okra and cook for 15 to 20 minutes more. Taste and correct the seasoning as needed and serve hot.

Crab Pickin, Sallie's Way

Blue crabs is very tasty, but if you don't know how to pick them (pulling the cooked meat from the bones) then you are in for a challenge. First remove the two claws. There is good meat in both parts of the claw that can be reached by cracking them with a mallet or heavy knife. Next remove the fins—or skinny legs, as I call them—from the shell. There is a little sweet meat in these, although some people just throw them away. Separate the crab from the bark (the shell), using your hand to pull it apart. Clean away and dispose of the spongy matter—the lungs and organ tissue—which sits on top of the crabmeat. Use your hands to break the crab in half; then I like to break each half in half again. To pick out the meat, you need to separate the bone from the meat. Use a knife or your fingers to do this. It's a process—eat as you go!

Another step in picking is to gather the crabmeat and sort through it, feeling for stray shells. If you've ever bought crabmeat at the store, you know what I mean. There are always bits of shell that have been missed in the picking process, and you don't want them in your food. Always look for "lump" crabmeat at the grocer, because that term means it has been picked through for shells already.

Coastal Grill Bass

Catching fish from our dock was a favorite pastime and meant we'd have a great meal that night. We would fish together as a family—Pop figured the more lines we had in the water, the more we'd catch!

Serves 4 to 6

1 teaspoon salt

1 teaspoon pepper

1 teaspoon garlic powder

1 (2- to 3-pound) whole bass, scraped and gutted

Lemon wedges, for serving

Combine the salt, pepper, and garlic powder and sprinkle over the entire fish, inside and out.

Heat a charcoal grill and spray the grill grate with nonstick cooking spray. When the coals turn white, place the fish directly on the grate and cook for about 3 minutes, then flip and cook for 3 minutes on the other side. Flip back to the first side and cook for 3 minutes, then to the other side and cook for 3 minutes. Repeat the turning and cooking on each side once more so that the fish is cooked for a total of about 9 minutes on each side for well-done. (For medium-well, cook on each side only twice for 3 minutes each.) Remove to a platter and serve hot.

Cast Nets

Pop was not born native of Daufuskie Island. He was born on Bull Island, a short boat ride away from Daufuskie. When he was young, around age eight, Pop's parents moved the family to Daufuskie, where his grandparents lived. Pop had several handicaps: he was blind in one eye and had one cripple foot. Never one day, however, did he allow his handicaps to hinder him doing his many challenging chores. Our rooster crowed early every morning, but Pop never laid in bed after the bird crowed.

He taught me and my siblings things we still appreciate today. Pop believed if something's worth doing, there's no reason you shouldn't try. Knitting a cast net was not easy to do and it took a very long time to complete one. Pop was really good at knitting shrimp and mullet cast nets, and sometime he would knit a net for other folks who paid him.

The time needed to make a cast net depends on how many hours you spend working on it every day. Pop often knitted at night as a way to get something else done before going to bed. After we finished our last evening chores, we all gathered in the living room; Pop would sit in a chair facing a corner of the room, knitting and telling stories about when he was growing up and about the many people who once lived on the island.

A cast net starts off with you putting a large nail in a wall or a tree. Then you make about thirty-two loops on the first row; each following row you knit makes the cast net wider and longer. Once you have made the size you want, you lay it out on a flat surface and put netting yarn in place from top to bottom. This netting is used to open and close the net when in use.

A cast net is used for catching fish and shrimp. First you need to find one for your size and feel. They come in various sizes—from four feet to six feet or ten feet. You will need the size that fits your height to be able to throw it properly. A cast net is also very heavy because of the metal ball weight that's added so that it sinks to the bottom when thrown out into the water.

Before throwing your cast net out, you tie the loop end of the long rope secure around your wrist. Then some folk place a piece of the net in their mouth and quickly release it when they throw so that the net spreads out when it hit the water. Other folks don't place a piece of the net in their mouth because they know how to spread their net using their hands and weight. Once the cast net sinks near or all the way to the bottom of the creek or river, the rope that's tied around your wrist is used to pull the cast net back in, closing it at the bottom and capturing what's been caught. Sometime you will get what you want, whereas other times you'll get nothing—or something you don't want.

Cast net knitting today is almost a lost art. A few of my siblings and I learned how to knit a cast net, but through the years, I didn't practice, and I forgot some of the steps. It was important to me to find someone to show me how to knit again, so I did. The gentleman who helped me learned from his father and was honored to show me. Most young folks today don't care to do the labor their parents or grandparents did, and I feel they are missing out on some of their heritage. Nowadays when I make the time, I work on knitting me a cast net even though I don't know when I will finish making it.

Island Fried Garlic Blue Crabs

Some people use gloves when they're breaking the crab shells because they don't want to touch the crabs, and it helps protect their hands from the sharp shells. It's your choice—we never used them, but I still occasionally get stuck by a shell while I'm picking crab.

Serves 4 to 6

2 cups vegetable oil

4 to 6 live blue crabs

2 to 3 teaspoons salt

2 to 3 teaspoons pepper

4 to 5 teaspoons garlic powder

Lemon wedges, for serving

Put the live crabs in a large stockpot, and carefully run enough hot water over them to slow them down so they won't hurt you as you work with them. Remove the claws from live crabs then debark and clean each one (see page 97 for instructions).

Heat the oil in a large skillet over medium-high heat.

Break each crab in half and season all over with salt, pepper, and garlic powder. Use tongs to carefully place about half of the crab pieces into the hot oil and fry for 3 to 4 minutes on each side, until brown. Remove and drain on paper towels and repeat the process until all the crabs are cooked.

Serve immediately, with lemon wedges.

From Earth to Plate

Springtime to me is the prettiest and best time of the year because it's when new life begins. Life springs from the soil, trees grow new leaves, flowers bloom all around you. For us, springtime was busy, breaking new ground for planting gardens or preparing some of the same spots year after year. Momma and Pop got excited as they pulled out their seeds saved from last year's crop, along with new seeds that they might have bought on a shopping trip over the water. Our garden was planned long before we dropped the first seed. Certain seeds had to be planted on a certain moon or tide so that the vegetables would grow their biggest and be plentiful.

Our corn grew tall, well over our heads, and when it was ready to pick we had to stretch up high on our tippy toes to reach the ears that was so sweet and juicy you could eat them raw. We all loved collards, which Momma grew in her garden or in a spot where she once had a pigpen. She said that the soil was much richer from their manure. The collard leaves grew wide and long there, with a deep rich green color, and next to them grew beautiful big heads of cabbage.

Momma loved all of her vegetables, and she made sure she had a section in the field left to grow her white potatoes and sweet onions that added so much flavor to many of the meals she prepared. When vegetables like cucumbers and tomatoes were ready for picking, some never made it in the house because we enjoyed the fresh taste of eating them right from the vine. Round, ripe cantaloupe and honeydew melons grew in the middle of the garden so that their vines would stretch across the field.

Watermelon was Pop's most favorite to grow. They were big ones, and some so large us girls couldn't pick them up alone. On a hot day Pop might go into the field and check to see which melon was ready for picking. Then he would bring his choice onto the front porch and send one of us girls to the kitchen for a big sharp knife. He would make sure he wiped the melon clean, and position it just right to cut and share. Our eyes would follow every move he made as he cut into the melon longways. The crisp sound and the sweet smell as he pulled the watermelon pieces apart made us very happy. We would hold our hands out as he cut, waiting for him to give each one of us a big slice. We would find a spot on the porch or the steps to sit and bite into the sweet melon. We didn't spit the seeds out, though. Sometime we would save the seeds for next year's planting, or we would throw the seeds to the chickens. They also liked picking on the rinds we threw out to them. Sometime Momma would save some of the watermelon rind to preserve and store with the rest of the vegetables and fruit for the cold winter months.

Squash, lima beans, and field peas grew plentiful, and we had more than enough to share with our family and neighbors. Sweet potato (tada) was a crop we planted twice; first the seedling was planted with the vegetable garden to grow the vines, and then the vines were cut and planted, which the sweet potato grew from. Tub or bushel baskets full of sweet potato would be collected, and some would go in the house in a dark corner or under the kitchen table in a box. They don't break down as quickly if they are kept in the dark. The rest would be buried in a hole covered with straw under an upside-down V-frame house in the backyard, to keep them safe to eat as needed during the winter months.

No matter how hard the gardening work was, we looked forward to the vegetables on our plates fulling our hungry bellies. Pop and Momma would always remind us that the food taste much better when you know the work you put into it. Those meals were the best. "Eat you vegetable," Momma use tah said, "cause yah grow and be smart and strong." Our hard work growing up gave me so much knowledge and bounty and pride for life. I'm forever grateful for that.

Tomato, Corn, Green Lima, and Okra Soup

I enjoyed growing vegetables, but okra was never my favorite—I don't like the smell. I include this recipe because it was our family favorite. My momma never made me eat it if I didn't want to, thankfully.

Serves 6 to 8

¼ cup vegetable or olive oil

1 to 1½ large onions, diced

1 quart chicken stock or water

2 teaspoons salt

2 teaspoons pepper

2 teaspoons dried or chopped fresh basil

10 to 12 large tomatoes, diced; or 2 (14.5-ounce) cans diced tomatoes

1 to 2 cups whole corn kernels cut from the cobs

1 to 2 cups fresh or frozen green lima beans

1 pound fresh okra, stemmed and cut into 3 pieces each

In a large soup pot, heat the oil over medium-high heat, add the onions, and stir for 2 to 3 minutes. Add the stock and bring to a boil. Add the salt, pepper, and basil, then stir in the tomatoes, corn, and lima beans. Cover and continue to cook over medium-high heat for 45 minutes to 1 hour, until the vegetables are tender.

Stir in the okra, decrease the heat to medium-low, and cook for 15 to 20 minutes, until the okra is tender. Serve hot.

Fresh String Beans with Tomatoes and Potatoes

This is really a vegetable soup and it's good in both summer and winter. Cornbread or biscuits are good to serve with this nourishing dish.

Serves 4 to 6

1 tablespoon vegetable oil

1 large onion, diced

5 cups chicken stock or water

10 to 15 fresh tomatoes, diced; or 2 (14.5-ounce) cans diced tomatoes

1 pound fresh or frozen string beans, cut into 2 or 3 pieces each

3 to 4 large white potatoes, peeled and cut into 1-inch chunks

1 to 2 teaspoons salt

1 to 2 teaspoons pepper

In a soup pot, heat the oil over medium-high heat. Add the onion and cook for 3 to 5 minutes, until translucent.

Add the stock and tomatoes, cover, and continue to cook over medium-high heat for 1½ hours, stirring on occasion.

Reduce the heat to medium and add the string beans, potatoes, and salt and pepper to taste. Cook for 35 to 45 minutes, stirring on occasion. Test to see if the potatoes are done to your liking, and cook longer if needed. Serve warm.

Steamed Fresh Lima Beans and Corn

Serves 6 to 8

2 cups fresh green lima beans

2 cups sweet corn kernels removed from the cobs

Salt and pepper to taste

In a steamer pot over medium heat, add 2 cups water to the bottom pot. When the water starts to boil, add the vegetables to the top. Season with salt and pepper, cover, and cook for 20 to 25 minutes, until the vegetables are tender. Keep an eye on the pot and add water as needed during the cooking. Serve hot.

Sautéed Cabbage with Sweet Onion

Serves 6 to 8

½ cup olive oil

1 cabbage, rinsed, drained, and cut into
2-inch pieces

1 sweet onion, sliced

1 to 2 teaspoons salt

1 to 2 teaspoons pepper

In a skillet, heat the oil over medium-high heat. Add the cabbage and stir-fry for 5 to 6 minutes, until lightly browned. Reduce the heat to low, add the onion, salt, pepper, and ½ cup water, and cook for 2 more minutes, stirring constantly. Serve hot.

Buttered Sweet Peas and Carrots

Serves 4

2 teaspoons butter

½ pound fresh or frozen sweet peas

½ pound fresh or frozen carrot pieces

¼ onion, diced

Salt and pepper to taste

Fill a medium saucepan half full of water and add the butter. Place over medium-high heat and stir to melt the butter, then add the peas and corn and cook for 20 minutes.

Reduce the heat to low and simmer for 10 minutes. Serve warm.

Sallie's Honey-Glazed Carrots

Serves 4

6 carrots, peeled and cut into 3 pieces each

2 tablespoons butter

⅔ cup honey

In a medium pot, bring 3 cups water to a boil over medium-high heat. Add the carrots and bring back to a boil. Cook, uncovered, for 10 to 15 minutes, until the carrots are tender but not mushy. Drain and return the carrots to the same pot. Decrease the heat to low and stir in the butter and honey until well blended. Serve warm.

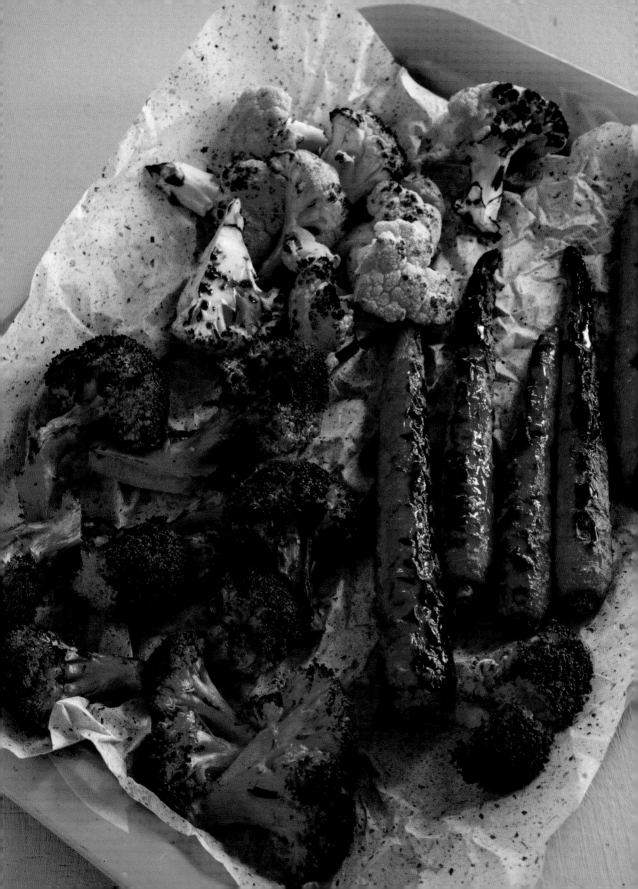

Grilled Broccoli, Cauliflower, and Carrots

Serves 4 to 6

1 head broccoli, cut into sections

1 head cauliflower, cut into sections

2 to 3 medium to large carrots, peeled and cut in half horizontally

Prepare a charcoal grill and light the fire. When your charcoal turns white, you are ready to grill.

Spray the grill grate with nonstick cooking spray. Place the broccoli, cauliflower, and carrots directly on the grill and cook for 1 to 2 minutes on each side, then repeat the process, until you see char marks on the vegetables.

Serve immediately.

Stew Tomato and Onion

Serves 4

1 to 2 tablespoons vegetable oil

1 large sweet onion, diced

8 to 10 ripe tomatoes, diced

In a large saucepot, heat the oil over medium-high heat. Add the onion and stir-fry for 3 to 5 minutes, until translucent. Stir in the tomatoes and 2 cups water, lower the heat to medium, and simmer for 15 to 20 minutes, stirring often. Add salt and pepper to taste.

Reduce the heat to low to keep warm until you are ready to serve.

Tomato, Okra, and Basil

If you like crispier okra, you can pre-fry the okra in a skillet with 2 tablespoons oil before adding it to the tomato sauce.

Serves 4 to 6

2 tablespoons vegetable oil

15 fresh tomatoes, diced; or 2 (14.5-ounce) cans diced tomatoes

1 heaping tablespoon tomato paste

1 teaspoon minced garlic

3 cups hot water

2 teaspoons salt, or to taste

2 teaspoons pepper, or to taste

4 fresh basil leaves

1 pound fresh or frozen okra, stemmed and cut into pieces

In a large saucepot, heat the oil over medium-high heat. Add the tomatoes, tomato paste, garlic, hot water, and salt and pepper to taste. Cook for 45 minutes to 1 hour, stirring often, until the sauce slightly thickens, and isn't watery. Reduce the heat to medium and stir in the basil and okra. Cook for 15 to 20 minutes more, checking to see you don't overcook the okra. Serve hot.

Black-Eyed Peas with Okra

Serves 6 to 8

1 pound dried black-eyed peas, rinsed and soaked for 15 to 20 minutes, then drained

Salt and pepper to taste

½ pound fresh or frozen okra, stemmed and cut into pieces

Fill a medium pot half full of water, add the black-eyed peas, and bring to a boil over medium-high heat. Cook for 1½ hours, stirring on occasion, until the peas are tender. If the liquid thickens, add more water, 1 cup at a time.

Once the peas are tender, lower the heat to medium, stir in the okra, and cook for 15 to 20 minutes, until the okra is tender. Serve warm.

Baked Squash and Zucchini

Serves 6 to 8

2 to 3 yellow squash, cut into 1-inch pieces

2 to 3 zucchini, cut into 1-inch pieces

2 to 3 medium to large carrots, peeled and cut into 3 or 4 pieces each

2 teaspoons salt

1 tablespoon pepper

1 tablespoon garlic powder

Preheat the oven to 350°F.

Arrange the vegetables in a baking pan in a single layer. Sprinkle with salt, pepper, and garlic powder and bake for 20 to 35 minutes, until tender. Serve warm.

Slavery

Among all the topics Daufuskie folks discussed and shared during their get-togethers, I never remember anyone ever holding conversation about slavery. It was as if certain things were not spoken of. My mom said she never knew anything about slavery, but knew of sharecropping when some folks use to plant on an area call Bloody Point. She said it was what folks did when they did not have enough land to plant on for themselves.

Sharecropping was when folks would plow, work, and harvest fields on the land of some who had large pieces of property; the owners of the property would get about half of the crop when it came harvest time. I grew up not knowing that there had been slaves on Daufuskie. After I left the island, I heard stories and got involved in learning more about my history and culture from way back yondah time. I have been told that Daufuskie was one of many islands that slaves fled to, but no one can recall who they were. Daufuskie today still has a few tabby ruins—shelters made from broken shells cemented together—at Haig Point plantation and other locations on the island that are said to have been slave or sharecropper quarters back in the day. Even though we roamed the island a lot when I was a child, I never knew the tabby ruins existed . . . I guess because our folks never mentioned them, and we never asked what those building made of oyster shell was. Maybe they felt we had so much ahead of us to be made aware of and that mattered more than bad memories of our ancestors' lives. Surviving on an isolated island without many amenities was hard enough. But even though I feel that those bad times wasn't talked about, they are not forgotten. Because it was those bad times that made it better for each generation after. And the more I learn about the struggle, the more I stand proud to be from the blood line of folks who believed, never gave up, and worked extra hard for me to have and do better.

Twice-Baked Potatoes

Serves 4

4 large white potatoes, skin on

1 to 2 teaspoons vegetable oil

4 slices bacon (optional)

1 heaping tablespoon butter

1 tablespoon minced garlic

1 teaspoon pepper

1 teaspoon salt

⅓ cup evaporated or low-fat milk

1 tablespoon chopped fresh parsley

2 tablespoons shredded cheddar cheese

Preheat the oven to 400°F.

Wash and pat dry the potatoes. Pour a little oil in your hand and rub each potato all over with oil, then wrap each in aluminum foil. Place in a baking pan and bake for 40 to 45 minutes, until tender.

While the potatoes are baking, fry the bacon until crisp, drain on paper towels, and crumble.

When they are done, cut each potato in half horizontally and scoop out most of the flesh into a medium-size bowl, leaving a thin layer of potato inside the skin so it holds its shape. Leave the oven on.

Add the butter, garlic, pepper, salt, milk, and parsley to the bowl with the potatoes. Use a masher or an electric hand mixer to mix well, then divide the mashed potatoes into 4 portions and use a large spoon to stuff it into the potato skins. (You can also put the mashed potato mixture in a pastry bag and pipe it into the skins.)

Sprinkle the potatoes with the cheese and bacon, place on a baking sheet, and bake for 5 to 10 minutes, or until the cheese melts.

These treats are best eaten hot.

Simply Fried Okra

Serves 4

2 cups vegetable oil

1 pound fresh okra, stemmed and cut into 3 pieces each

1 teaspoon salt

1 teaspoon pepper

1 cup cornmeal or self-rising flour (or ½ cup of each, mixed)

In a skillet, heat the oil over medium-high heat until hot, but not smoking.

Put the okra in a bowl, sprinkle with the salt, pepper, and cornmeal (or cornmeal-flour mixture), and toss to coat evenly. (Alternatively, put the ingredients in a large plastic or paper bag, and shake to coat.)

Shake off any excess cornmeal, then carefully place the okra in the hot oil using a slotted spoon. Cook for 3 to 4 minutes total, turning to lightly brown all over.

Use the slotted spoon to remove the okra and drain on paper towels.

Serve hot.

Bigotry

I had never heard the word *bigotry*, or understood what it meant, until I left the island where Gullah folks and about five white families lived in harmony and mutual support.

For many years, Daufuskie Islanders have been the subject of stories and rumors told by folks off the island . . . folks who saw our way of life as strange. These folks would tell made-up stories to impress, or frighten, or just gain attention. This is how some bigotry starts: from folks who lie about the truth or refuse to accept people of other nationalities or religions.

Such was the situation one day many years ago when tourism on Daufuskie was new, and ferries from the mainland to Daufuskie began to bring day visitors over. I caught one of the tourist boats going back to Daufuskie from Hilton Head and had my first rude awakening to some of the things that were being said about my people.

The captain of the boat must have thought it would be interesting to tell his crowd of all-white passengers some stories about the native people on Daufuskie. (I'm sure he did not know that a native-born Gullah was also riding on the boat that day; when I had boarded the boat, I picked a spot in a corner so that I could enjoy the view.) As soon as he piloted the boat away from the dock, he began to share information about Hilton Head and Daufuskie while the passengers talked and gazed. As we crossed the Calibogue Sound near Daufuskie, he spoke about some of the history of the first point of the island, which was Haig Point. Then, as we came around the last bend of the island and approached the dock where we were going to get off, he began to talk about the folk who lived on Daufuskie.

As I listened to what he was saying I couldn't believe my ears. At first, he told some history of the people on the island who had first been brought from Africa to work on the rice plantations; then, out of the blue, he said that if his passengers met a native it would be best not to talk with them. The reason he gave was that they spoke a language no one could understand (half true; as I mentioned earlier in the book, the Gullah language was invented by slaves so they could talk among themselves without the slave owners knowing what was being said).

Then he crossed the line and said that the natives lived in huts up in the trees, were basically wild, and wore bones in their noses. By now, most of them was oohing and aahing.

As for me, I was feeling like a blowfish out of water. I felt like going up into the captain's booth and giving him a piece of my mind. Instead, I took a deep breath and shouted out, "Why is dis yah man telling dese people lies on us?" Immediately all heads turned and stared at me, as I turned with my back to them. The captain heard me and said, "Oh, I guess I am in a little trouble."

I was so mad I couldn't wait to get off dat boat as we were docking. When a lady asked, "Miss, can I ask you a few questions?" I turned and said, "I am not here to make trouble, but dat captain needs to tell yall dah truth. Ma'am, I was born and raised on Daufuskie, do I look like what he described?" She shook her head, looking a little ashamed, and said, "No you don't." She wanted to ask me more questions, but I told her I would rather she go on the tour first. I told her I would talk to her once she was back at the building where I would be serving their lunch. She thanked me and was pleased to know that she would get the opportunity to talk with a native again.

We got off the boat and I went on with my business, getting their lunch together, while the group got on a bus and went on their tour. Afterward, she came to me and said it was a beautiful island and that she and the other tourists had seen other residents who looked normal. She was in disbelief that the captain would say such things about folks that was not true. I told

her that it was my first time hearing what was said. All I could think of was he was making money off folks who did not know what to expect, coming to a small undeveloped island like Daufuskie.

After that day I was still upset and felt I had to do something more. I knew that if this is what folks that day was being told, I could only imagine what else was being said. I heard other folks saying that they had heard similarly strange things said about us, and I decided maybe I should write about the real way of life on Daufuskie—explaining that our life was no different from others except we was not in a hurry to go places, or in need of things yesterday instead of today. We lived in peace, free from running over others to get where we were going. For some folks that may have been their past, but to us it was our life, and we didn't need lies and tall tales passed on as jokes just for the fun of it.

Being from a small, undeveloped island you could only reach by boat did not mean we were wild or had bones in our noses. As born natives of Daufuskie, we were proud folks and loved others for who they were. We did not judge one another by the color of their skin, or what they didn't have. That knowledge makes me proud, and it's something they should try.

Collard Greens & Cabbage with Smoke Neck Bones

Many folk have never combined these two vegetables, but they go together well. Crunchy cabbage and silky collards are complementary flavors and textures.

Serves 8 to 10

3 pieces smoked pork neck bone (or smoked turkey wings)

1 small bunch collard greens, picked over (remove any dead leaves), destemmed, and cut into 2 or 3 pieces

1 large sweet onion, diced

1 small cabbage, cut into 2-inch pieces

1 tablespoon salt

1 tablespoon pepper

Fill a large pot half full of water, add the smoked neck bones, and bring to a boil over medium-high heat. Cook for 25 to 30 minutes, then drain off the water and return the meat to the pot, along with 3 cups hot water, and bring to a boil again. Cook for 20 to 30 minutes.

While the meat is cooking, wash the collard leaves several times in warm water, and drain in a colander.

When the meat is almost tender, add the collards and the onion. Season with salt and pepper, decrease the heat to medium, cover, and simmer, stirring on occasion, for 1 hour. Next add the cabbage and more water if needed, and cook for 30 to 45 minutes, until the cabbage is as tender as you like it.

Keep warm over low heat until ready to serve. Serve with the cooking liquid, or potlikker.

Green Lima Beans with Ham Hocks

Some people use ham hocks just for flavoring, as in this recipe, but we Gullahs like to eat the smoked pork. If you don't like pork you can substitute smoked turkey wings or beef stew meat. Note: Soaking dry lima beans first will make them cook a little faster.

Serves 6 to 8

3 to 4 smoked ham hocks, cut in half (ask your butcher to cut them) or smoked turkey wings

1 onion, diced

1 pound dried green lima beans

1 teaspoon pepper

1 teaspoon salt (optional)

Soak the lima beans in a bowl with enough water to cover the beans for 30 to 45 minutes.

Put the ham hocks in a large pot and cover with water. Bring to a boil over medium-high heat and cook for 1 hour, then drain the pot, reserving the ham hocks, and add enough water to fill it half full. Return the ham hocks to the pot, along with the onion. Drain and rinse the beans and add them to the pot with the meat. Season with salt and pepper, stir, and cover. Cook over medium-high heat for 2 hours, or until the beans are tender, stirring on occasion and adding more water if needed. Serve hot.

String Beans, Smoke Turkey Wings, and White Potatoes

Serves 6 to 8

3 to 4 smoked turkey wings

1½ pounds fresh string beans, snapped

1 onion, diced

4 large white potatoes, peeled and cut in half

Fill a large pot half full of water, add the smoked turkey wings, and bring to a boil over medium-high heat. Cook for 45 minutes, then drain off the water, and again fill the pot half full of water. Again bring to a boil and cook another 45 minutes. At this point, the turkey wings should be a little tender.

Lower the heat to medium, add the string beans and onion, stir, cover, and cook for 30 minutes, or until the string beans are tender.

Add the potatoes and continue to cook over medium heat for about 20 minutes. Serve hot.

Rutabaga and Smoke Neck Bones

Rutabagas are a hard root. In order to remove the skin, cut the top and bottom off, then cut it in half through the middle. Lay the halves flat on a clean surface and use a sharp knife to remove the skin; cut into 1-inch-thick pieces, then dice.

Serves 6 to 8

4 pieces smoked pork neck bone

1 smoked ham hock, cut in half (ask your butcher to cut it)

2 rutabagas, peeled and diced (see note)

Salt and pepper to taste

In a large stockpot, combine the neck bone and enough water to half fill the pot. Bring to a boil and cook for 30 to 40 minutes, then drain. Again fill the pot half full of water, add the neck bone, and bring to a boil again, then add the rutabagas and salt and pepper. Lower the heat to medium and cook for 1½ hours, stirring on occasion, until the rutabagas are tender. You can eat them as is, or you may choose to use a potato masher and mash them in the pot.

Serve the rutabagas with the neck bones.

Rice Dishes

To our ancestors who worked long, hard hours growing and picking rice in fields on Daufuskie and elsewhere in the South, I thank you. Even though during my childhood we did not plant it like our ancestors before us, we ate rice almost every meal. Rice is a starch that has been gracing tables for more than eight thousand years, tracing back to ancient China. Today it is cooked thousands of ways, in delicious cultural dishes across the world. I enjoyed many rice dishes growing up, and to this day I continue to cook and share the rice dishes of my ancestors of long ago. These Gullah recipes add great flavor to rice, using meat, seafood, and seasoning.

Bacon, Eggs, and Rice

This is great for breakfast, lunch, or dinner. It's a quick, tasty, and filling meal.

Serves 4

1 cup long-grain white rice

2 teaspoons salt

6 to 8 slices bacon

4 to 5 eggs

1 teaspoon pepper

In a medium pot, rinse the rice several times, and drain. Add 1½ cups water to the pot, along with 1 teaspoon of the salt, then stir, cover, and cook over medium heat for 45 minutes, or until the grains are loose, not sticky.

Preheat the oven to 350°F.

Arrange the bacon on a half sheet pan, or flat pan with low sides, so grease doesn't spill out. Bake for 5 to 8 minutes, or until the bacon is crispy, then transfer to paper towels to drain, leaving the grease in the pan.

Break the eggs into a bowl and stir in the remaining 1 teaspoon salt and the pepper.

Add 2 tablespoons of the bacon grease to a medium skillet over medium-high heat, add the eggs, and scramble to your desired doneness, stirring constantly.

Remove the skillet from the heat and add the bacon crumbles and rice and gently toss to combine.

Serve warm in bowls.

Stew Chicken and Rice

This is a favorite Sunday supper or potluck dish. You'll enjoy the leftovers, too.

Serves 6 to 8

1 (3- to 5-pound) chicken, cleaned and cut into pieces

½ cup vegetable oil

1 large sweet onion, diced

½ green bell pepper, diced

½ red bell pepper, diced

1½ ribs celery, diced

2 teaspoons crushed or minced garlic

6 cups hot chicken stock or water, or more if needed

2 teaspoons salt

1 tablespoon pepper

1 teaspoon dried or fresh thyme

1 tablespoon poultry seasoning

3 cups long-grain white or jasmine rice, rinsed and drained

Wash and pat the chicken pieces dry.

In a large soup pot, heat the oil over medium heat. Use tongs to carefully place the chicken pieces in the hot oil, and cook for 4 to 5 minutes on each side, until slightly browned.

Drain most of the oil from the pot, leaving about 1 tablespoon, and add the onion, bell peppers, celery, and garlic to the chicken. Cook over medium heat for 1 to 2 minutes, tossing constantly, then add the hot stock, the salt, pepper, thyme, and poultry seasoning and stir. Cover the pot partially, leaving a slight opening, and bring to a boil. Continue to cook for 1 hour and 45 minutes, stirring on occasion, until the chicken and vegetables are tender. Check the stock for seasoning.

When the chicken is fork tender, use a slotted spoon to transfer the pieces from the pot to a pan, and carefully remove and discard the skin and bones. Return the chicken meat to the pot.

Preheat the oven to 350°F.

Add the rice to the chicken pot, stirring well to combine. If needed, add ½ to 1 cup more stock for the rice to cook—you don't want mushy rice.

Transfer the mixture to a large baking pan or aluminum pan, cover, and bake for 45 minutes to 1 hour. Uncover and stir, cover again, and cook for another 35 to 45 minutes. Keep warm until you are ready to serve.

Back in dah Day Gatherings

Wherever I've lived, when I mention I am from Daufuskie it never fails to start a conversation. Some people remember in the mid-1960s to the early '70s riding over to Daufuskie on Captain Sam's boat called the *Waving Girl*, a party boat that could hold 250 people or more.

Captain Sam would make his Daufuskie boat runs on Friday, Saturday, Sunday, and sometimes at night from May through September, and the island natives would prepare a feast of our famous deviled crabs, boiled shrimp and crab, and homemade plum and grape wine for the visitors. Us kids would boil peanuts and pick plums and grapes to help out.

Folks would pack the boat for the slow cruise from Savannah to Daufuskie, dancing to the music of James Brown, Aretha Franklin, Otis Redding, the Temptations, and others. As the boat cruised toward Daufuskie at night, we could see its lights and hear the loud music as it slowly moved through the channel from miles away. There were no electric lights at the dock, so folks brought flashlights and flambeaux to show the food they had for sale there. As soon as the boat docked and all lines were secured, the crowd would race off the boat, piling around each table to buy the tasty island goodies. After making their purchases, some folks would take a walk down the dirt road, while others gathered in a concrete building we called The Club. They could dance to music played on a "picalow" (our name for a jukebox). Forty-five minutes or an hour was all they got on land before the boat horn was blown for everyone to return to the boat. Folks would party all the way back with the best of soul music, food, and fun.

All that great Daufuskie food that the island natives had prepared would usually be sold that night, and natives would return home in their ox- or horse-pulled wagons to plan for the next night or day that the boat returned.

'Fuskie Fried Crab and Shrimp Rice

Serves 6 to 8

1½ cups long-grain white rice

1 teaspoon salt

4 tablespoons vegetable oil

3 slices bacon

⅓ green bell pepper, diced

⅓ red bell pepper, diced

½ rib celery, diced

1 large onion, diced

4 ounces lump crabmeat

4 ounces claw crabmeat

½ pound medium-size raw shrimp, peeled and deveined

1 tablespoon minced garlic

Salt and pepper to taste

In a large stockpot, wash and drain the rice several times, then add 2½ cups water and the salt. Stir to combine, cover, and cook over medium heat for 30 to 45 minutes, or until the rice is tender.

In a large skillet over medium heat, fry the bacon until crisp. Remove from the skillet and set aside, leaving the bacon grease in the pan. Add 2 tablespoons oil to the pan, along with the bell peppers, celery, and onion, and cook for 3 minutes, or until the vegetables have softened. Transfer the vegetables to a bowl and set aside.

Add the remaining 2 tablespoons oil to the skillet over high heat, then add the crabmeat and sauté, stirring occasionally, for 3 to 5 minutes, until the crabmeat begins to brown. Add the shrimp and the rice to the crabmeat, and stir together for 2 minutes, or until well combined and the shrimp is cooked through.

Stir the sautéed vegetables and the garlic into the rice and heat through. Season with salt and pepper.

Serve hot in bowls.

Smoke Neck Bones and Rice

Smoke pork neck bones were once called "poor folks' food" because they have very little meat on the bone. If you have not had them, this recipe will surprise you. There may not be much meat, but there's more than enough good flavor in them bones. You can find them in most groceries in the pork section, or at your local butcher.

Serves 6 to 8

2 pounds smoked pork neck bones

1 large onion, diced

1 teaspoon pepper

1 tablespoon vegetable oil

1 teaspoon salt

2½ cups long-grain white rice, rinsed and drained

Add the neck bones to a large pot, along with enough water to cover by at least 1 inch. Bring to a boil over medium-high heat, cover, and cook for 30 minutes, then drain off the water, and fill the pot half full of hot water. Add the onion, pepper, and oil and bring to a boil again; cover and cook for 1 hour, or until the meat is tender enough to fall off the bones.

Add the rice to the pot with the neck bones, and more water if needed (it will take about 3½ cups water to cook the rice properly). Stir, reduce the heat to medium, cover, and cook for 1 hour, stirring on occasion, until the rice is tender.

Alternatively, you may bake the rice mixture in the oven for the final hour of cooking. Pour the mixture into an aluminum pan or baking dish, cover, and cook at 350°F for 1 hour, then uncover, stir, and taste for seasoning. Cover, and cook for another 25 minutes, if needed, and serve hot.

Gullah Oyster Rice with Shrimp

The instructions may seem to call for a long cooking time for the oysters and shrimp, but they are mainly a flavoring ingredient for the rice.

Serves 6 to 8

3 to 4 slices bacon

2 tablespoons vegetable oil

2 tablespoons self-rising flour

1 large onion, diced

½ green bell pepper, diced

½ red bell pepper, diced

1 tablespoon minced garlic, or ½ tablespoon garlic powder

Salt and pepper to taste

1½ pints raw shucked oysters, drained

½ pound small raw shrimp, peeled and deveined

2 cups long-grain white rice

Preheat the oven to 365°F.

Fry the bacon in a large pot or Dutch oven over medium heat until crisp, then remove and set aside, and drain off all but 2 tablespoons of the bacon fat.

Return the pot to medium-high heat, add the oil and flour to the bacon fat, and stir constantly until the flour turns a medium dark brown color. Add 5 cups water, the onion, bell peppers, and garlic. Bring to a boil over medium heat, cover, and continue to boil until the gravy slightly thickens. Add salt and pepper to taste, then stir in the oysters and shrimp and cook for 10 to 15 minutes.

Wash and drain the rice twice, then add to the pot. Stir to combine, then transfer the rice mixture to a baking dish or aluminum pan. Cover and bake for 1 hour or more, stirring on occasion, until the rice is tender. Serve hot.

'Fuskie Favorite Red Rice with Sausage and Beef

Red rice was and still is a favorite at traditional Sunday dinnas, funerals, and family reunions. Red rice is made many ways, passed down through generations of cultures from all over the world. This Gullah version has sausage and beef added, which makes it different from meatless southern versions.

Serves 8 to 10

2 tablespoons vegetable oil

4 slices smoked bacon

1 pound pork or beef sausage links, cut into ½-inch-thick rounds

1 large onion, diced

½ pound ground beef

½ green bell pepper, diced

½ red bell pepper, diced

1 rib celery, diced

1 teaspoon dried thyme

1 tablespoon minced garlic

2 (14.5-ounce) cans diced or stewed tomatoes, with juice

2 tablespoons tomato paste

8 cups hot water

Salt and pepper to taste

1 teaspoon sugar

3 cups long-grain white rice

In a large pot, heat the oil over medium-high heat. Add the bacon, sausage, and onion and sauté for 1 to 2 minutes. Remove from the pot, leaving the bacon fat. Add the ground beef to the pot and fry for 3 to 4 minutes, until loose and brown, then return the onion mixture to the pot.

Add the bell peppers, celery, thyme, garlic, tomatoes, tomato paste, hot water, and salt and pepper. Stir well to combine and simmer for 20 to 30 minutes, stirring on occasion, until the mixture starts to thicken. Stir in the sugar to balance the tartness of the tomatoes. Cook for another 30 minutes, stirring on occasion, to thicken some more.

Wash and drain the rice twice, then add to the sauce and combine well. Cover and cook, stirring on occasion, over medium-low heat for 1 hour, or until the rice is tender. Serve warm.

RED RICE COOKED IN THE OVEN

If you prefer to cook the rice in the oven, preheat the oven to 350°F.

In a large pot, heat the oil over medium-high heat. Add the bacon, sausage, ground beef, and onion and sauté for 1 to 2 minutes. Add the bell peppers, celery, thyme, garlic, tomatoes, tomato paste, hot water, and salt and pepper. Stir well to combine and cook for 20 to 30 minutes, stirring on occasion, until the mixture starts to thicken. Stir in the sugar to balance the tartness of the tomatoes. Cook for another 30 minutes, stirring on occasion, to thicken some more.

Wash and drain the rice twice, then add to the sauce and combine well. Transfer the mixture to an aluminum foil baking pan or casserole dish, stir, and cover. Bake for 20 to 30 minutes, then check the rice, stir and cover again, and bake for 30 to 40 more minutes, until the rice is tender. Serve warm.

Fried Fish and Rice

This fish dish is a popular lunch or supper on Daufuskie.

Serves 4 to 6

2 cups long-grain white rice

2 teaspoons salt

2 cups vegetable oil

4 to 6 fish fillets (whiting or trout)

1 teaspoons pepper

3 teaspoons garlic powder

1 cup self-rising flour

Put the rice in a large pot, and rinse and drain several times, then add 3 cups water and 1 teaspoon of the salt, stir, and cover the pot. Cook over medium-high heat for 1 hour, then reduce the heat to very low to keep warm.

In a large skillet, heat the oil over medium-high heat.

Meanwhile, arrange the fish on a clean surface or a sheet pan and season on both sides with the remaining salt, the pepper, and garlic powder.

Put the flour in a large resealable bag (or a paper bag), then add the fish fillets and toss to coat well. Shake off any excess flour and carefully place the fish fillets, three at a time, in the hot oil to fry. Cook for 3 to 4 minutes on each side, or until the fish is browned. Use a spatula to carefully transfer the fish to drain on paper towels. Repeat until all the fillets are cooked. Serve over the rice.

Mixed Vegetable and Rice

Serves 4 to 6

1½ cups long-grain white rice

2 tablespoons butter

1 onion, finely diced

¼ red bell pepper, finely diced

¼ green bell pepper, finely diced

1 cup fresh or frozen corn kernels

1 cup fresh or frozen shelled sweet peas

1 to 2 teaspoons salt

Rinse and drain the rice several times and set aside.

In a medium pot over medium heat, melt the butter, add the onion and bell peppers, and cook for 1 to 2 minutes, stirring. Add the corn, peas, salt, and 2 cups water, and stir to combine. Cook for 10 minutes, then stir in the rice, cover, and cook for 1 hour, stirring several times to keep the rice from clumping, until the rice is tender.

Serve hot.

Down Yondah Beef and Rice

Beef for us was "the other meat." We ate beef less then we ate other proteins like pork, chicken, and fish. This dish was a great treat for us.

Serves 4 to 6

3 teaspoons salt

2 teaspoons pepper

1 pound beef stew meat

2 tablespoons vegetable oil

1 tablespoon self-rising flour

1 onion, chopped

1½ cups long-grain white rice, rinsed twice and drained

Sprinkle 2 teaspoons of the salt and the pepper over the beef cubes and toss well to coat on all sides.

In a large skillet, heat the oil over medium heat, add the flour, and stir continuously until it turns brown. Add the onion along with 3 cups water, and stir continuously for 2 to 3 minutes. Add the rice and the remaining 1 teaspoon salt, stir, and cover the pan. Reduce the heat to low and cook for 1 hour, or until the rice is tender.

Serve hot.

Beenyah's Seafood Fried Rice

This dish tastes like a fancy meal, with all the rich seafood added. To us, it was just another of Momma's great creations using whatever she had on hand at the time.

Serves 8 to 10

6 slices bacon

1 large onion, sliced into thin strips

½ green bell pepper, sliced into thin strips

½ red bell pepper, sliced into thin strips

2 tablespoons vegetable oil

½ pound lump crabmeat

½ pound claw crabmeat

1 cup raw shucked oysters, drained

½ pound small raw shrimp, peeled and deveined

Salt and pepper to taste

2 to 3 cups cooked rice

Fry the bacon in a large pot over medium-high heat until crisp, then remove and drain on paper towels, leaving the bacon grease in the pot.

Add the onion and bell peppers to the pot and stir-fry for 3 to 4 minutes, until the onion is translucent. Remove the vegetables, again leaving the drippings in the pot.

Add the oil and the lump and claw crabmeat and fry, stirring, until slightly browned, then add the oysters, shrimp, and salt and pepper and cook for 3 to 5 minutes.

Reduce the heat to medium and stir in the rice and vegetables. Crumble the bacon on top and serve.

Momma only fixed desserts for us on Sundays and holidays, which was a big treat. The Sunday sweets never lasted through the week, of course. Holidays were the best because we had more than one dessert and could make them last longer. Holiday desserts were usually sweet potato pie, bread pudding, and blackberry dumplins—heaven in a kid's eyes.

Southern Treats Double Piecrust

Piecrust is basic and very easy to make. I suggest doing it yourself by hand, but you can choose to use a food processor. Good prepared pie dough is available at your grocery, but when you make your own, you know there are no preservatives in it, which I like.

Makes enough for 1 (9-inch) double-crust pie, or 2 (9-inch) single-crust pies

2 cups all-purpose flour

¾ teaspoon salt

1 stick chilled butter, diced

3 to 4 tablespoons shortening (Crisco or lard, but not oil)

6 tablespoons cold water

Put the flour and salt in a medium mixing bowl, then cut in the butter and shortening and blend together using your hands, until the dough is coarsely mixed. Add the cold water and continue mixing gently with your hands until the dough holds together in one mass.

Divide the dough into two equal portions. Roll each portion out on a clean, lightly floured work surface to a disk ⅛- to ¼-inch thick.

To make a double-crust pie: Press one disk evenly into a pie pan, with enough dough to hang over the edges. Add your pie filling and top with the second disk. Seal the edges by crimping them with your thumb and forefinger all around. Use a fork to pierce the top of the crust, and bake as directed.

To make a single-crust pie: Press one disk evenly into a pie pan, with enough dough to hang over the edges; trim and crimp the edge. Put the second crust between two sheets of waxed paper, cover with aluminum foil, and freeze to use for your next great pie.

To prebake a single-crust pie shell: Preheat the oven to 350°F. Place the dough-lined pie pan in the oven and bake until lightly browned, then remove from the oven and let cool completely.

Holidays, the Daufuskie Way

New Year is supposed to be the time of year you can start to make things better with a clean slate, letting go of the old and welcoming in the new. Folks on 'Fuskie would cook up many of our traditional dishes along with a few sides to celebrate on New Year's Eve. Right as the clock struck midnight, with the old year going out and the new one coming in, we would get on our knees and give thanks for the blessings of old things the year had brought.

The traditional dishes, cooked by everyone, included collard greens (which was said to bring more money in the New Year) and red peas and rice cooked together (said to bring good luck). There was always a pot of hog chitlins, which didn't have a meaning that I can remember, but was loved by most as a holiday treat. Desserts like bread pudding (page 156) and sweet potato cornbread (page 165) we never tired of enjoying.

Holidays on Daufuskie were very happy times when most folks got together for the occasions. Big meals, sometimes ten or twelve items on the table, were normal for folks to cook and share. Natives would start gathering ingredients weeks in advance because some items had to be brought from over on the mainland. Other ingredients came from our backyards or had to be caught, hunted, or processed before the big day. Momma and other Gullah cooks didn't think it was right and proper to set a holiday feast without one or two wild game dishes, yard-raised meats, fresh or preserved garden vegetables, fresh seafood caught from the river, and several kinds of sweet treats for dessert.

Even though we went to church most Sundays, we really looked forward to Easter service. The cold weather was gone and the feel of warmer weather was welcome. Spring was showing off with the beautiful bright colors of wildflowers and the new leaves covering trees that were recently bare. The air felt lighter, and we knew it wouldn't be long before we could go barefoot in the sandy roads. We kids would spend countless hours at school and at home practicing our Easter speech (usually about Jesus), to be delivered later at the church Easter program.

Come Easter morning, we would rush to do our chores early so that we could dress up in our Sunday best. Momma would have washed, starched, and ironed our outfits and made them look like new. And we couldn't wait to show them off as we stood in front of everyone to say the speech that we worked so hard to learn. While the service was going on, several folks would be hiding the Easter eggs outside for us to find later. The most exciting part of the hunt would be finding the golden egg and getting a prize.

With such a big family as ours, there were so many birthdays that we didn't celebrate them because we knew that the family did not have the money to buy each of us gifts or do something special for each one of us every time we had a birthday. Pop would say, "You

(continued)

(continued)

need to thank dah Lord for allowing you to see another day." And we were happy just to be fed and have each other to share all that we had. Years later when I left Daufuskie and I was a parent, I made myself a promise that, no matter what, I would treat myself on my birthday . . . and I do.

Even though we were told in school what the Fourth of July meant, we really weren't aware of how big a holiday it was for most Americans, and little celebrating was done on island. Certainly no fireworks, or anything like that.

Halloween was the first big fall holiday, and every year our parents and other islanders would come together and have a Halloween party at the school for all the children. Our house on Daufuskie was not next door or close to others like folks' homes were on the mainland, so trick-or-treating was out . . . and, in any event, our parents were not going to let us run around unsupervised just to collect candy after dark.

Thanksgiving was turkey day, just like in the rest of the country, and time was up for one of the big turkeys that ran around the chicken yard or roamed around the house feeding on the grass. Momma would choose which one's time was up. We would all have our chores to help her prepare for the big day, making lots of other great treats that we couldn't wait to eat.

This time of year was also hog-killing time, when Momma would need to clean the chittlins for a special dish. I was her helper and I hated that job. Hog head cheese was another particularly popular pickled delicacy—some people call it "souse." Other great dishes were an annual tradition on the island—wild game, such as raccoon, baked or stewed; fried rabbit; or roasted deer ham, the hind leg of a deer. Helping out with all this meant that there was a lot more work for us kids to do, but we never complained because we knew how delicious the reward was going to be. Lots of food was cooked, but none of it was wasted. Momma would often pile up a plate high for us kids to deliver to folks who did not have family members, or were sick and shut in. And you can imagine how great the leftovers were.

The year was winding down and the last big holiday, Christmas, was only weeks away. At school, we kids would make lots of Christmas decorations from pinecones that we gathered and decorated with strips of paper to make a chain for our Christmas tree. Many of the decorations would be hung around the house or put on the pine tree that would be cut from the nearby woods. Everyone on the island prepared in one way or another for the day to come. The celebration of Christmas actually lasted for a week, which meant that a lot of work had to be done around the house because of all the family and visitors who would be coming and going. Sometimes folks would come across from the mainland just to celebrate with us, because they knew the fun we were going to have.

For days, Momma, like all the women, cleaned and got ready to cook. Folks would be dropping by throughout the week to eat, sing, shout, and reminisce about Christmases past. A big shopping day was planned a week or two in advance, and a large boat hired from Savannah would take everyone who wanted to shop to and from the mainland. Sometimes the shopping list would include a new piece of furniture or an appliance that had been saved up for all year.

As kids in our house, we knew that if nothing else, we were going to get new clothes and shoes as presents. Most of the time we didn't expect to get any toys because we knew money was tight and our needs were more important and came first. For some folks on the island, Christmas was the only time they would leave their home to visit others.

From Christmas Day until the New Year, walking from house to house to visit others on the island was a tradition. Tables were set with fruits, candy, cake, homemade wine, liquor, and in the kitchen pots would line the woodstove with some of each family's best food. Visiting someone on Christmas meant you had to eat or drink something off the table before leaving to visit the next house. You might join in singing an old spiritual song, which often led to shouting and laughter. Folks, black and white, celebrated together, and no one was disrespected or turned away. I still miss those wonderful days when we were all one and sharing from the heart, because it was all about being together on the island we called home.

Blackberry Dumplins

This is a very special and easy dessert. Momma would make this for us after we spent hours picking blackberries, making all the work worth it.

Serves 4

1 pound fresh or frozen blackberries

2 cups sugar

Dough:

1½ cups self-rising flour

½ teaspoon salt

1 teaspoon sugar

3 tablespoons shortening (Crisco or lard, but not oil)

¼ to ¾ cup cold water

Put the blackberries and sugar in a medium saucepot with 1 cup water and bring to a boil over medium heat. Cook for 3 to 4 minutes, stirring, until it thickens to a sauce. Reduce the heat to low and keep the blackberries warm as you make the dough.

Make the dough: In a large mixing bowl, stir together the flour, salt, sugar, and shortening with ¼ cup cold water. Add more water, up to ¾ cup total, as needed until the dough is loose and soft enough that you can scoop it out with a spoon.

Increase the heat under the blackberry pot to medium.

Scoop 1 teaspoon dough at a time and drop it into the saucepot of blackberries. When the dough rises to the top of the blackberry sauce, use a tablespoon to turn it so the dough cooks evenly as it hardens. Drop in as many teaspoons of dough as you can at the same time, but leave a little room between them for the dough to swell. When all the dough is turned and the dumplings have the consistency of doughnuts, the blackberry dumplings are ready to eat.

Momma's Pecan Pie

Everyone had pecan trees on the island, so this was a popular dessert in the fall and during holidays. My grandmother would get the grandkids and we would gather pecans for her. She had nine trees, and there were so many nuts she would bring them to the Savannah market to sell.

Serves 6 to 8

Dough for 1 (9-inch) single-crust pie (page 146)

½ cup (1 stick) butter, melted

1 cup light brown sugar

1 cup dark corn syrup

¼ teaspoon salt

3 large eggs, beaten

1½ teaspoons vanilla extract

2 cups chopped pecans

Prepare the piecrust and put it into a pie pan as directed in the recipe.

Preheat the oven to 350°F.

In a large bowl, combine the butter, brown sugar, corn syrup, salt, eggs, and vanilla.

Place the pecans in the bottom of the piecrust. Pour the egg mixture over the pecans. (The pecan pieces will float to the top.) Bake on the bottom rack of the oven for 1 hour, then move to the top rack and bake for another 5 minutes, or until it browns on top. Let cool completely, then slice and serve.

Simply Strawberry Ice Cream

The heavy cream makes this ice cream fluffy and fabulous. You'll want to make this treat often during the summer months.

Serves 8 to 10

2 pints fresh strawberries, washed and hulled

¾ cup sugar

1 cup heavy cream

Put all the ingredients in a food processor or blender and blend until smooth. Pour into a bowl, cover, and freeze for 2 hours, removing the bowl from the freezer every 30 minutes and stirring to distribute the fruit well. When the ice cream is firm, transfer to a lidded container and freeze. The ice cream will keep for up to 5 days (covered) in the freezer. If it lasts that long.

Sweet Baked Candy Yams with Pineapple

When Momma had extra cans of pineapple, she would add it to her candied yams. It makes the yams even sweeter than they already are and makes for an easy, quick dessert.

Serves 4 to 6

6 sweet potatoes, washed, peeled, and cut into quarters

1 pinch salt

1 cup canned pineapple pieces, with the juice

½ cup (1 stick) butter, cut into small pieces

½ cup light brown sugar

1½ teaspoons vanilla extract

1 teaspoon ground cinnamon

1½ teaspoons ground allspice

1½ cups granulated sugar

Juice of 1 lemon

1½ cups orange juice

Preheat the oven to 350°F.

Put the sweet potatoes in a pot with salted water to cover and bring to a boil over medium-high heat. Cook for 30 minutes, or until the tadas are tender but still firm, then drain and place in a casserole dish. Pour the pineapple pieces with juice into the casserole.

In a medium bowl, combine the remaining ingredients and mix well. Pour over the tadas. Bake for 1 hour, basting with the juices several times during cooking.

Serve in a bowl or dish, and spoon the sauce from the casserole dish over each serving.

Momma's Pineapple Bread Pudding

Bread pudding will rise during the baking time, and when you remove it from the oven it will fall a bit. Don't worry—this is normal and doesn't affect the taste.

Serves 8 to 10

1 loaf white or wheat bread (day-old is best)

1 cup (2 sticks) butter or margarine, melted

1½ cups sugar

5 large eggs, beaten

2 to 3 cups whole milk

1 cup evaporated milk

1 tablespoon vanilla extract

½ teaspoon ground cinnamon

2 teaspoons ground allspice

4 (8.5-ounce) cans crushed pineapple, with juice

Preheat the oven to 350°F.

Tear each slice of bread into 5 or 6 pieces, place in a bowl, and set aside.

In a separate large bowl, combine ¾ cup of the butter with the sugar, eggs, 2 cups whole milk, the evaporated milk, vanilla, cinnamon, and allspice. Mix well until the sugar dissolves, then stir in the pineapple and juice.

Gently fold the torn bread into the liquid ingredients, making sure the bread soaks up the liquid ingredients. If the mixture seems dry, add a little more milk.

Divide the remaining butter between two 9-by-13-inch baking pans or casserole dishes, coating them well. Place the pans in the oven for a few minutes to heat. Remove the pans from the oven and pour equal amounts of the bread pudding mixture into the pans. Bake, uncovered, for 1½ to 2 hours, until the bread pudding is browned on top and a toothpick inserted in the center comes out clean. Let cool slightly, then serve.

Rum Cake

This isn't a kids' dessert. Momma never served it at our house. I learned to make this after I grew up and left home. It's a very moist cake, and it will stay moist. I wish I could tell you how long it will keep, but it never lasts at my house more than a couple of days.

Serves 8

1 teaspoon shortening, to grease the cake pan

5 large eggs

1½ cups sugar

2 teaspoons vanilla extract

½ cup (1 stick) butter, melted

2½ cups all-purpose flour, plus 1 tablespoon more to flour the cake pan

2 teaspoons baking soda

1½ cups light or dark rum

Topping:

½ cup powdered sugar; or powdered sugar icing (2 cups powdered sugar mixed with ¼ cup/½ stick melted butter)

Preheat the oven to 350°F.

Lightly grease and flour a 10-inch Bundt pan or 9-inch tube cake pan.

In a large bowl, beat the eggs with a hand mixer on medium speed while gradually adding the sugar. Then add the vanilla, butter, flour, and baking soda and gently mix on low speed. Finally, mix in the rum.

Pour into the cake pan, leaving about 1 inch of space at the top. Bake for 45 to 50 minutes, until the top is golden brown and the cake has slightly pulled away from the edge of the pan. The cake is done when a toothpick inserted into it comes out clean. Set the cake aside to cool slightly before removing it from the pan. Let the cake cool completely.

Dust with powdered sugar, or ice with powdered sugar icing, then serve.

Easy Fixin Peach Ice Cream

This is a recipe Momma used to make. We kids would gather on the front or back porch and hand churn the ice cream—a chore that taught us that somehow hard work would always reap good rewards! Today we have gadgets that help make things easier and faster in the kitchen. That's all good, but the lesson has been lost.

Serves 6 to 8

4 to 6 ripe peaches, peeled and cut into pieces

¾ cup sugar

1 cup heavy cream

Put all the ingredients in a food processor or blender and blend until smooth. Pour into a bowl, cover, and freeze for 2 hours, removing the bowl from the freezer every 30 minutes and stirring to distribute the fruit well. When the ice cream is firm, transfer to a lidded container and freeze. The ice cream will keep for up to 5 days (covered) in the freezer.

Peach Upside-Down Cake

Momma had a way of knowing how to make a little bit of something into a great meal—and we were happy that this talent extended to desserts, too. Sometimes it would be from a little of this or a little of that but, nevertheless, by the time she got through with her mixing and fixing, no one ever left the table hungry.

Serves 6 to 8

Cake:

½ cup (1 stick) butter, softened

1 cup sugar

2 large eggs, beaten

2½ cups all-purpose flour

1¼ teaspoons baking powder

1½ teaspoons vanilla extract

½ cup milk

½ cup peach juice (reserved from the glaze below)

1 (20-ounce) can sliced peaches, plus the juice from the can (reserve ¼ cup of the juice for the glaze)

Peach Glaze (recipe follows)

Preheat the oven to 350°F.

In a large bowl, mix the butter and sugar using a hand mixer on medium speed, until smooth and light. Add the beaten eggs slowly, then add the flour, baking powder, vanilla, milk, and ½ cup reserved peach juice, and mix until the batter is smooth.

In the bottom of a 9-inch round cake pan, sprinkle some of the batter, then lay the peaches evenly on top. Pour the remaining batter over the peach slices and bake for 35 to 45 minutes, until a toothpick inserted in the middle of the cake comes out clean.

Invert the cake onto a serving plate and allow the cake to cool for 30 minutes after you remove it from the pan. At that point, use a tablespoon to drizzle the glaze over the top of the cake, allowing some to drip down the sides.

Peach Glaze

¾ cup (1½ sticks) butter

⅔ cup light brown sugar

¼ cup peach juice reserved from the canned peaches

In a skillet, melt the butter over low heat and add the brown sugar and peach juice. Cook for 6 to 8 minutes, stirring continually, until the sugar is dissolved.

Country Pear Pie

Pear pie is pretty much like apple pie except you need to cook the pears much longer. It is as delicious as apple pie—maybe more so. And, just like apples, you can never have enough. If you cook a batch of pears, you can make preserves out of the extra, or freeze them to use later. Make sure you use hard pears; soft pears won't do. Use more or less sugar depending on how sweet you like your pie.

Serves 6 to 8

15 to 20 hard pears, peeled, cored, and cut into wedges

4 to 5 cups sugar

1 teaspoon ground cinnamon

½ teaspoon ground allspice

½ teaspoon grated nutmeg

½ teaspoon ground cloves

Grated zest of ½ lemon

Dough for 1 (9-inch) double-crust pie (page 146)

Put the pears in a large saucepot over medium heat. Stir in the sugar, cinnamon, allspice, nutmeg, cloves, lemon zest, and 1 cup water. Cover and cook for 2 hours, stirring on occasion. The pears will turn reddish as they soften while cooking. You can cook the pears to a firm or soft texture—your choice. Taste when the pears are done in case you want to add a little more spice. Set the cooked pears aside to cool (be very careful: the syrup is very hot and a little sticky).

Prepare the pie dough and put the bottom crust into a pie pan as directed in the recipe.

Pour the filling into the piecrust and cover with the second round of piecrust, crimp the edges together to seal, and pierce the top with a fork. Bake for 30 to 40 minutes, or until the crust has lightly browned. Let cool, then slice and serve.

Note: Hard pears may take several hours to cook but are well worth the time.

Homemade Strawberry Pie

Serves 6 to 8

Dough for 1 (9-inch) single-crust pie (page 146)

Pie filling:

2 pints fresh strawberries, washed, hulled, and halved, plus more for garnish

Strawberry Glaze (recipe follows)

Whipped cream, for garnish

Preheat the oven to 350°F. Prepare the pie dough and put the crust into a pie pan as directed in the recipe. Bake it, unfilled, for 20 minutes, or until browned. Set aside to cool slightly.

Put the strawberries in a medium bowl. Add the strawberry glaze (recipe follows) and mix well. Transfer to the prebaked pie shell, piling the fruit high in the middle. Use a spoon to smooth the top. Refrigerate for 30 to 45 minutes or more before serving. When you are ready to serve, top with whipped cream and strawberries.

Strawberry Glaze

1 pint fresh strawberries, washed, hulled, and sliced

½ cup sugar

1 tablespoon cornstarch, dissolved in 3 tablespoons cold water

In a small pot over medium heat, combine the strawberries, sugar, and cornstarch mixture and bring to a boil. Cook for 4 to 6 minutes, stirring continuously. Let cool completely.

Pecan Sour Cream Pound Cake

Get out a large bowl, and get busy! This is easy and good.

Serves 8 to 10

Nonstick baking spray or oil or Crisco and flour, to coat the cake pan

2 cups sugar

4 large eggs, beaten

2 teaspoons vanilla extract

1 tablespoon freshly squeezed lemon juice

2 cups sifted self-rising flour

¾ cup (1½ sticks) butter, melted

1 (8-ounce) tub sour cream

2 cups pecan pieces

Preheat the oven to 350°F. Use non-stick spray or grease and flour to coat a 10-inch Bundt pan or 9-inch tube pan.

In a medium bowl, combine the sugar, eggs, vanilla, and lemon juice and mix well. While still stirring, gradually add the flour, butter, sour cream, and pecans until well combined.

Fill the prepared pan three-quarters full, leaving room for the cake to rise. Bake for 45 to 55 minutes, until a toothpick inserted in the cake comes out clean. If needed, bake a little longer, in 5-minute intervals, until done. Let cool in the pan. Remove from the pan, then slice and serve.

Sweet Potato Cornbread

Oh, how I remember those days when it was time to harvest the sweet potatoes and cook them. So many different dishes! And as simple as it may sound, this recipe was a favorite in our house.

Serves 8 to 10

1 teaspoon salt

4 to 5 sweet potatoes, skin on, cut into 3 pieces each

4 cups yellow self-rising cornmeal

1 cup self-rising flour

3 large eggs, beaten

2 cups whole milk

1 cup evaporated milk

1½ cups sugar

2 teaspoons vanilla extract

1 cup molasses

1 cup (2 sticks) butter, melted

Preheat the oven to 350°F.

Half fill a large pot with water and add the salt and sweet potatoes. Over medium-high heat, bring to a boil and cook for 30 minutes. The potatoes will still be firm. Drain and set aside to cool, then peel them.

In a large bowl, combine the cornmeal and flour.

In a medium bowl, combine the eggs, whole milk, evaporated milk, sugar, vanilla, molasses, and ¾ cup of the butter. Using a hand mixer on medium speed, or a spoon, mix well until the sugar is dissolved. Fold in the sweet potatoes.

Fold the dry ingredients into the wet ingredients and combine well. Try not to break up the sweet potatoes.

Add the remaining ¼ cup butter to a 9-by-13-inch baking pan or a large skillet, and place in the oven until hot.

Pour the batter into the heated pan, leaving ½ inch of space at the top for room to rise. Bake for 45 minutes to 1 hour, until the top is slightly browned and a toothpick inserted in the center of the cornbread comes out clean. Let cool, then slice and serve.

Blueberry Pound Cake

Wild blueberries grew in many places on Daufuskie, and still do. The wild berries are more tart than sweet, but we loved them and would race to see who could pick the most.

Serves 8 to 10

1 cup light brown sugar

¾ cup (1½ sticks) butter or margarine, softened

3 large eggs, beaten

1 teaspoon vanilla extract

½ cup milk

2½ cups all-purpose flour

1½ teaspoons baking powder

¼ teaspoon salt

2 cups fresh blueberries

½ cup powdered sugar

Preheat the oven to 350°F. Spray a 9-inch tube pan or 10-inch Bundt pan with nonstick baking spray.

In a medium bowl, combine the brown sugar, butter, eggs, and vanilla and use an electric mixer to beat until smooth. Add the milk and blend.

In a separate medium bowl, combine the flour, baking powder, and salt. With the mixer on low speed, gradually add the dry ingredients to the egg mixture and mix until the batter is combined. Fold in the blueberries.

Pour the batter into the prepared pan; gently shake the pan to level the batter. Bake for 45 minutes to 1 hour, until a toothpick inserted in the center of the cake comes out clean. If you check the cake as it bakes, remember to open and close the oven door gently.

When the cake is done, set the pan aside to cool a bit before removing it from the pan. Let the cake cool completely. Sprinkle with powdered sugar just before serving.

Sweet Tada Pound Cake

Sweet potatoes grew well in my parents' garden, and we loved to eat it in desserts or as a side dish.

Serves 8 to 10

Oil or Crisco and flour to grease and flour the pan

3¼ cups self-rising flour or cake flour

½ teaspoon grated nutmeg

½ cup light brown sugar

1 cup granulated sugar

½ cup milk

1 teaspoon vanilla extract

5 large eggs, beaten

¾ cup (1½ sticks) butter, softened

6 to 8 sweet potatoes, peeled, boiled, and mashed

Preheat the oven to 350°F. Grease and flour a 9-inch tube pan.

Put all the ingredients in a large bowl and blend with an electric hand mixer on medium speed until the batter is smooth and well combined.

Pour the batter into the prepared pan and bake for 50 to 55 minutes, until a toothpick inserted in the center of the cake comes out clean. Let cool slightly before you remove from the pan. Let cool completely, then slice and serve.

Gullah White Potato Pie

Many of you have had and made sweet potato pie and love it. If you have, it's time to try what my Grandmomma used to make with white potatoes.

Serves 6 to 8

Dough for 1 (9-inch) piecrust (page 146)

5 to 6 large russet potatoes, peeled, cooked, and mashed

¾ cup (1½ sticks) butter, softened

2 cups sugar

4 large eggs, beaten

1 teaspoon ground cinnamon

1 teaspoon ground allspice

½ cup sweetened condensed milk

½ cup whole milk

Preheat the oven to 350°F.

Prepare the piecrust and put it into a pie pan as directed in the recipe.

In a large bowl, use a hand or stand mixer on medium-high speed to combine the mashed potatoes, butter, sugar, eggs, cinnamon, all-spice, sweetened condensed milk, and whole milk. Beat for 5 minutes, until the texture is smooth. Pour into the piecrust and bake for 35 to 45 minutes, until the top is lightly browned. Let cool, then slice and serve. Taste the flavor of sweetness and love.

Acknowledgments

The dedication for my book calls to my ancestors, and I would like to acknowledge them all here, starting with my great-great-great-grandparents Joe Fields (born 1830) and Ceily (Sara) Brown. They were the parents of Lydia Fields (1850–1940), who married Henry Green William (born 1849). They became my great-great-grandparents and had thirteen children, and among them was daughter Sally (Sarah) Williams (1882–1957), whom I am named after. Sally (Sarah) married Charlie Bentley and they became my great-grandparents and had six children. Their oldest became my grandmother, Louvenia Bentley (1897–1982). She married Josephus Robinson (1900–1997), who was one of sixteen children born to Sue Robinson and Sipio Robinson (1822–1895), also my great-grandparents. My grandparents Louvenia Bentley Robinson and Josephus Robinson had six girls who gave them forty-four grandchildren (about seven died at birth). One of their six children was my mother, Albertha Robinson Stafford (1928–2013), who later married my stepfather Thomas Stafford Sr. (1920–1988). Mom passed while I was writing this cookbook and is deeply missed by everyone whose path she crossed and who ate at her dinna table for any occasion but most of all to get a bellyful.

These are the folks who loved life and gave all they could, paving a way so that I could share with you the wonderful memories of down-home goodness that has graced many mouths and sustained many lives since long before I was born. The stories are as real as yesterday when I relive each moment of back-in-dah-day, enjoying the memories of the best years of learning things from the past and how to make do with it in my future.

This book contains treasures from the hearts and minds of many ancestors who served up belly-fillin meals with so much love; they are long gone but will never be forgotten, with countless memories to be proud of and to carry on their legacy and mine to come. They were the ones who planted the seeds for my future. They gave their best and tried their hardest to instill in us things they knew from their own past experience, and about things they learned along their own way, so that we could do and have better than they did.

My stepfather Pop used to say, "I may be dead and gone but y'all chillin will see what I'm talkin bout, a hard head makes a soft behind. Learn ta listen and become a leader and you will go far in dissha world, cause you can't live in it by yo self. But what you gotta do first is wake up every day and you will learn something." Oh, those words didn't mean much then, but today I understand what he was saying. I value his teaching and tough love more than he will ever know.

Folks didn't mind working from dawn to dusk with pride in themselves, taking each challenge one day at a time with a grain of salt. Each task was the start of a new beginning, of getting things done, and a pathway for those who were yet to come. Their love, respect, and commitment were about family and the way of life they were living. Having manners and showing respect for all others came from having morals learned at an early age. Folks believed that you have to teach a child from the time they were born into this world, not when they are old enough to make decisions on their own. There's no mountain too high nor valley too low to keep you from achieving success if you give it your all—which is why giving up when times get hard is not an option.

Here is what this all means in my native Gullah tongue:

As I look back on dem good ol' day, a place, way, and time where I grew up wit so many treasured memories bout good organic food, hard work, a carin commun'ty, tuff love, an much faith and full bellies . . . I be joyful.

I thank dose folks whom taught me to enjoy one day at a time and don't dwell on what I can't change but to move forward cause life comes wit joy and pain. For me dey fought dah battle for better, now I just have to keep winning dah war fo more greatness.

My life is because of strong folks before me of long ago dat helped made 'em possible so dat I (we all) can be all dat we want to be cause dey cared enuff bout us to pave dah way.

Many thanks to my siblings who pointed out that what we think we know as kids doesn't compare to the lessons we learn along our way.

I'm proud to be the parent of son Jermaine Adonis Robinson and his wife Kecia Polite Robinson; daughter Rakenya Niccole Robinson; son Isiah Lamar Coleman; and son Thomas Morris Bush. They have given me so much joy and a heap of grandkids to love every day and to carry on for generations to come.

Always remembering first-born son, Charles Edward Simmons IV, who passed at age six (in 1981), and the loss of my sister Sylvia Williams (2013) and younger sister Lois Fay Robinson (2017).

I am grateful for my grandkids, who teach me new things while I teach them old ones: Jaquasha Anreona Bush-Bonaparte and husband Desmond; Jermaine Adonis Robinson Jr.; Charmaine Jamira Robinson; Tanashia Arielle Robinson; Janaesha Kiona Robinson; Isiah Lamar Coleman Jr.; Ivery Coleman; Amarion Bush; Savion Bush, Treveon Bush, Jasmine, TJ and Dijanae Polite-Moody and husband Marquis.

Much love and thanks to my agent and editor, Janice Shay, for being supportive, understanding, and patient while I wrote this cookbook; for the great photography by Deborah Whitlaw Llewellyn; for the gorgeous styling and props by the great food stylist and author Annette Joseph.

Wesley and Carrie Campbell helped make

these recipes a success—from their fresh fruit, vegetable, and seafood market locations on Hilton Head Island, Bluffton, and Daufuskie Island (on Saturday only). And when I am in Savannah I sometimes go to Nelson Quality Shrimp in Thunderbolt, where I get to sometimes see my friends Nelson and Jay unload hundreds of pounds of freshly caught shrimp—and I can't help but to bring some home. Many more thanks to Deborah Smith, owner of Daufuskie Rental Group, who helped set up a lovely place to shoot the food photos. Thanks to Sage and Bethany for use of their lovely cottage 118 in Melrose, where I cooked and the photos were taken. I thank all my families, friends, and neighbors on Daufuskie and around the world for your love and support.

I am so thankful to my higher power for the blessing of being who I am as I walk through my life journey, hugging and sharing happiness everywhere I go.

Glossary of Gullah Words and Phrases

I have written some of the text in *Sallie Ann Robinson's Kitchen* in my native Gullah dialect because dats the way I learned to cook. My grandmother, my parents, and some of our neighbors spoke Gullah when I was a child, but we never knew or heard the word *Gullah* at the time . . . it was just the way we spoke. It wasn't until I moved away to the mainland to continue my education that I discovered that the way I spoke was a different dialect. I felt embarrassed about being teased and didn't understand why, so I had to learn to speak slower and pay more attention to how I said my words. I am very proud that we now have a Gullah Bible written in both Gullah and English. I don't speak Gullah as fluently today as I did growing up, but some of the more common Gullah words I grew up with, and their meaning, are contained in this glossary and appear in the stories for you to experience and enjoy.

Afta = after—I will call the kids afta I get back from ovar yondah.

Ansa = answer—I always ansa wit a smile.

Beenyah = born native/been here—I am a beenyah from Daufuskie Island.

Befo = before—Befo I go, I will walk the dog.

Betta = better—Life was betta on Daufuskie.

Bout = about—It's all bout you.

Cept = accept—It is okay to cept dah tings dah do.

Chillen, churn = children—There are three chillen at my house.

Comeyah = someone that live in a place where they were not born—They are comeyah people.

Cuppa = cup of—Two cuppa sugar, please.

Dah = the—Dah food is cold and need warming.

Dare = there—I'll be dare fo you.

Dat = that—I have been dare and done dat.

Dawfuskie = an early spelling of Daufuskie (Island).

Dem = them—I am going ovar da to see dem.

Den = then—Den you are dah one.

Dese = these—Dese are dah way I like it.

Dey = they or there—Dey are my pride and joy.

Dinna = most times, the third meal of the day—Dey is nuttin like a great meal fo dinna.

Dissha = this—Dissha is dah way it is.

Enuff = enough—I have had enuff of your talkin.

Famemba = to remember—I famemba dah good old days.

'Fuskie = Daufuskie Island—My home.

Fo = for—I will be dare fo you.

Gullah = first the name of our language, then defined as our way of life.

Gwaine = going—I will be gwaine on my way.

Heapin = a lot of—You be in a heapin trouble.

Humney = food or meal—Time for humney.

Hunah = a person—Who is dat hunah ovar dare?

Hungree = hungry—I'm hungree.

Iffa = if—Iffa you don't move otta my way, dah will be trouble.

Justa = just the—It's justa way it is.

Mattar = matter—Everything mattar now.

Mo = more—I would like to have some mo, please.

Mout = mouth—We both have a mout full of food.

Nuttin = nothing—It ain't nuttin but love.

Ovar dah = over there—I will be going ovar dah when yah come.

Sallet = salad—You have got to taste my tada sallet.

Shrew = through—Sometime you just got to go shrew it to understand.

Starten = starting—You are just starten to understand what I mean.

Sumting, sumptin, sumpin = something—Tell me sumting good.

Tadas = potatoes, white, red, any color—Bring me dah tadas.

Tings = things—It was fun the way we did tings.

Tink = thank or think—Tink yah fo bein dare.

Undah = under—Look undah dat table.

Wachin = watching—I'll be wachin you.

Wit = with—I want to be wit you.

Yah = you—Yah need to go wit me.

Yo = your—Dissha yo toy?

Index

Page numbers in *italics* indicate illustrations.

SALLIE ANN ROBINSON was raised on Daufuskie Island and is a sixth-generation Gullah native. She is a renowned chef, caterer, and tour guide in the Savannah and Sea Islands region.

Her first two books are *Gullah Home Cooking the Daufuskie Way* and *Cooking the Gullah Way, Morning, Noon, & Night*. She is also coauthor of *Daufuskie Island* with Jenny Hersch.

Robinson has appeared on the Food Network and the Travel Channel, ETV, and GPB, and she was also invited to the Smithsonian National Museum of African Art to talk about and cook a Gullah feast. Robinson was a student of Pat Conroy's when he taught at the island's schoolhouse (his book about this experience, *The Water Is Wide,* was made into the movies *Conrack* and *The Water Is Wide*). Pat died in 2016 and is truly missed, leaving a big void. His legacy lives on and continues to grow by many he inspired. Because as we live each day we all have a story to tell.

WITHDRAWN